C000154699

More Ramblings
of a Rustic
Copper

Brian Walter Wood

First Published in 2015
by Write Now! Publications
14 Hambrook Close,
Gt Whelnetham,
Bury St Edmunds,
Suffolk IP30 0UX

**All the stories in this publication are true with the
exception of a couple which I have put in Italics. However
some of the other stories have been slightly modified to
give a more coherent picture of the circumstances.**

**Where I have referred to other police officers or members of
the public, in most instances I have used a fictitious name
to prevent embarrassment or distress**

ISBN: 0957020214
ISBN-13: 978-0-957020214

ACKNOWLEDGMENTS

I would like to thank my daughter Carolyn for her patience and encouragement whilst I was writing this book. I would also like to thank Jez Reichmann for his help with the artwork, formatting the book and to Shiona Rolfe and Gerry for the many hours spent proof reading and correcting the errors.

Without their help this book would not have been published.

In memory of my good friend Cyril Wise.

MORE RAMBLINGS OF A RUSTIC COPPER

INTRODUCTION

In my first book, 'The Ramblings of a Rustic Copper' I related stories of my police service, firstly with the Buckinghamshire Constabulary then with the Thames Valley Police. About my rocky start when a sergeant tried his hardest to drum me out whilst I was a probationer, my early beat experience in Aylesbury, a further eight years with the Traffic Department, promotion to sergeant with a posting to the City of Oxford, then finally my exploits as a detective sergeant with the Motor Vehicle Investigation Squad.

In the final paragraph of that book I made the observation that no doubt further ramblings would come to mind in due course, well, that prediction proved to be true, so here we go with 'More Ramblings of a Rustic Copper'.

In this book I have referred to various crimes and scams committed by thieves and fraudsters. I would like to stress that all of these events occurred before 1986 and since then organisations such as the police, the DVLA and the insurance industry have tightened up their security and computer systems so these crimes today would be quickly solved.

All of the stories in this book are true but to protect the sensibilities of some of the characters mentioned I have altered their names somewhat, and occasionally I have enhanced the truth slightly to make the stories more readable.

HIGH WYCOMBE

I joined the Buckinghamshire Constabulary on the 14th March 1955 and after three months training at Eynsham Hall near Witney, Oxfordshire; my first posting in mid-June 1955 was to High Wycombe.

During my first months in uniform I formulated in my mind what I would like to do during my police service. I wanted to serve as a beat officer for five years, five years on the Traffic Department, five years on CID and my final fifteen years as a village constable, preferably in one of those small villages in the Chiltern Hills or in the Vale of Aylesbury. Promotion then was not an option.

Little did I realise that events over the next thirty years of my police career would be vastly different to what I planned.

My time at High Wycombe was short and of no real

consequence, as on the 9th August 1955 I married Gerry and then applied for a police house.

From August until the end of October 1955 we lived apart, I was in lodgings at 63 Green Street, High Wycombe and Gerry lived with her parents in Leighton Buzzard, Bedfordshire.

Even then, on my days off, due to shortage of room I spent my rest days at my parental home, Cherry Orchard Farm, Stockgrove, about five miles from where my wife lived in Leighton Buzzard. We were eagerly looking forward to being allocated a police house.

AYLESBURY

In October 1955 I was allocated a police house at 83 Stoke Road, Aylesbury. This was a dingy, two bedroom house, originally owned by the LMS Railway Company, condemned by them as not fit for human habitation so it was bought by the police!

83 Stoke Road did not have any heating or a hot water system, it was damp and cold with an outside toilet, but it was our first house and we were grateful of the chance to be together, at last.

The house was enhanced somewhat when Gerry's parents bought us a roll of linoleum to cover the flagstones in the kitchen/scullery. We were really going up-market.

Initially, the only furniture we bought was a bed but our families and friends donated various other items of furniture and crockery. To make it cosier during the cold evenings Gerry and I used to make Readicut rugs.

I used to go to the local woods to scavenge for fallen branches, saw them into logs, and this was our heating system.

At Aylesbury my shift sergeant was Jim Mellows, an ex-Coldstream Guards Sergeant Major, a man who could only be described as formidable. I am sure most probationers were terrified of him, I certainly was, but also admired him.

He was a strict disciplinarian but totally fair. He was hard as nails but when necessary he would show compassion and kindness. He was a good role model of what a policeman should be and I hoped that some of his qualities would rub off on me during my probationary period.

THE LAZY MENTOR

At Aylesbury, my mentor was a copper of the old school. I reckon he had joined the police before World War Two, he was a lazy so and so.

He said to me "To be a good copper you have to practice invisibility." I was obviously bemused by this comment, he then enlightened me, "A good copper knows where the deep recessed doors are, the quiet alleyways and the small shops where you can sneak in to get a cuppa tea, you see, if the public cannot find you they cannot lumber you with their problems."

On another occasion he said, "If I feel energetic I found the best thing to do was to lie down until the feeling goes away."

Did I heed his advice and practice invisibility? Well no, generally speaking I believe I carried out my duties with due diligence but I do admit that when I was cheesed off or felt I had been put upon I did take my mentor's advice, practice invisibility and sneak away for a quick (or sometimes slow) cuppa.

FROM POLE TO POLE

Shortly after my posting to Aylesbury I was soon to be aware there was a problem with DP's, in other words Displaced Persons, Poles. No, not bits of wood but people from Poland.

During and after World War Two there had been a large influx of Polish people to England and Aylesbury had its fair share.

These people were required to have ARC's (Alien Registration Certificates) and if and when they moved from town to town they had to register their movements at the respective police station so we always knew exactly how many were registered in Aylesbury.

In fact there were four problems, the first was that due to their language we could not understand them, and they were disinclined to learn English, and unbelievably none of the constables at Aylesbury spoke Polish. The second was that due to the language problem they were unemployable, they had nothing to do except on Thursdays. This was the third problem as it was on this day that they collected their dole money but with nothing to do it seemed like the vast majority of them spent their time in the pubs and got drunk. The fourth problem was their surnames, they were all W's, S, C's and Z's so even if we knew their names we could not pronounce them.

About twenty to thirty of these DP's, all men, lived in Nissan type hut accommodation in Rabans Lane, off the Bicester Road, Aylesbury, and then there was another camp on the old Wing Airfield about five miles away and some of those occasionally made their way into Aylesbury to partake of alcohol and get more than a little merry.

There was a story, or perhaps a legend, that in the earlier days after World War Two there was a parish south of Aylesbury called Walton and this parish was divided from the parish of Aylesbury by a small stream. A constable manned each parish.

One late afternoon the Aylesbury parish constable found the body of a gentleman dead in the stream against the Aylesbury bank. He recognised him as a Polish gentleman reputedly known as a habitual drunkard and as it was a Thursday he assumed the man in a drunken stupor had fallen in the stream and drowned.

What to do? He knew what he should do faced with the task of recovering the body from the stream, getting the handcart and conveying the body to the mortuary (in those days the ambulances would not carry dead bodies). Arrange a post mortem and then notify the coroner and there would have to be an inquest; establish identification and then notify next of kin, the constable took the easy way out. He got a long pole from a nearby clothesline and pushed the body across the stream to the far bank and into the parish of Walton. He had poled the Pole.

Shortly after, a member of the public told the Walton constable about the body in the stream. After seeing it and coming to the same conclusion as to the man's death and facing the same problems he thought, hang on a minute, no Poles live in my parish, this is Aylesbury's problem, so he took the same line of action and poled the body back to the Aylesbury bank.

Stalemate was reached but it was soon resolved. The two constables, after a short conversation, and with their respective poles, poled the Polish gentleman's body downstream out of their parishes and into the parish of Stoke Mandeville. Problem solved.

Now this does sound like a lot of old cobblers but having met some of those old parish constables who served during and after World War Two I know some may have looked for the easy way out of work, so there may be an element of truth in this story.

BERTIE THE BANK ROBBER

When I left Aylesbury Police Station at 10pm in early December 1955 it was bitterly cold, I was not looking forward to spending four hours walking the beat. Thankfully I was wearing pyjamas under my uniform.

About twenty minutes into my patrol I was in Kingsbury Square when I heard a crash of glass coming from the Market Square area, I ran there and saw that one of the windows of Lloyds Bank had been smashed and a man with a brick in his hand was hammering at the front door of the bank. I said to him.

"What do you think you are up to?"

Quite a silly question really to which he replied,

"Trying to get into the bank to steal some money," the man answered.

I said,

"You can't do that it's against the law and you are under arrest."

I then arrested him and walked down to the police station, there was no need to handcuff him, as he appeared pretty harmless.

On the way I had a startling thought, I, an almost new probationer constable had just arrested an armed (with a brick) bank robber! Whew. In those early days it was only senior detectives who arrested bank robbers.

Inspector Cameron was called out to hear the evidence and accept the charge and to have the prisoner placed in the cells. Meanwhile, for one hour of my patrol time I was in the comparative warmth of the police station.

It was a feeble attempt by Bertie to try to break into the bank and I knew, as did the Judge at the Quarter Sessions, that Bertie's futile attempt at robbing the bank was no more than a ruse to get himself into prison and out of the cold for the duration of the Christmas period where he would be provided with a Christmas dinner.

Bertie's efforts were successful and he was sentenced to three months imprisonment.

THE HAPPY DRUNK

It was another week of 10pm to 6am duty, and another cold night. Around 10:40pm I heard discordant singing coming from the vicinity of Temple Square.

There I found this happy drunk called Sam singing his heart out, bless his little cotton socks, staggering along the pavement. When he fell into the road I considered him to be drunk and incapable so for his own safety I arrested him, took him to Aylesbury Police Station and put him in a cell to sober up.

Sam was well known in Aylesbury as he had been arrested quite frequently for being drunk and incapable.

The next morning I roused him from his slumbers and as it was decided not to charge him I released him from custody. As I was doing so the following conversation took place, I asked,

"You were well under the weather last night, what were you celebrating?"

He replied,

"I have no idea, I have a bad memory."

Then to keep the conversation going I asked,

"What will your wife say because you did not go home last night?"

He replied,

"She will probably assume I had forgotten where I lived, it's my memory you see."

This was getting ridiculous so I asked,

"Is your memory that bad?"

To which he replied,

"Yes, she is a good wife, every morning when I wake up the first thing she does is to remind me that my name is Sam."

I am still unsure whether or not he was pulling my leg; at least he was not a troublesome drunk.

As I watched him leave the police station, he turned left, walked a few paces stopped, looked bewildered, then turned round and wandered off in the opposite direction. As he wandered down the road I wondered, will he find his way home or is he still today looking for where he lived?

VERBOSITY AT ITS BEST

Constable Ted Jeakins was a somewhat verbose young constable and he could talk the hind leg off of a donkey, as the saying goes. This trait was reflected in his somewhat flowery reports, as this little story will demonstrate.

Working the town centre on a 2pm to 10pm shift, he found to his horror that he had lost his warrant card. This was a serious matter; if the warrant card ended up in the wrong hands the finder could use it for ulterior purposes.

Ted reported the loss to his sergeant who told him to submit a written report about its loss to the superintendent. Now that report recorded chapter and verse practically every step Ted had trod, every person he had spoken to and every action taken that afternoon.

His sergeant added a submission note to the end of this massive missive that was of several pages, and then it was transmitted upwards to the superintendent.

Superintendent Bill Tomlin was man of few words, he endorsed the report in red letters: "FIND IT," and sent it back to Constable Jeakins.

All that fine prose was wasted on the superintendent.

The warrant card was not found or handed in by a member of the public and Constable Jeakins was disciplined and fined.

I recall on another occasion when Ted was in verbal full flow, his Sergeant Paddy Murnane said to him, "We have two ears and one mouth so that we can listen twice as much as we speak."

Good advice, but alas it made no difference to Ted.

Sergeant Paddy must have known his Greek classics as it was the Greek Philosopher Epictetus who around 100 AD uttered the above words of wisdom.

THE TRAMP

For the ten years that I was stationed at Aylesbury I knew about the tramp that visited the town in late November every year.

He came along the A41 from the Bicester direction and settled in the hedgerow about a mile or so outside the town.

He arrived pushing a pram that contained his worldly belongings. Despite the rain, snow or frosty nights he slept in the same spot under the hedgerow. He used to put a tarpaulin on the ground, wrap himself in his clothes and then with another tarpaulin over the top he was reasonably snug in his cocoon.

On more than one occasion I know he was offered sheltered accommodation that he politely declined.

Aged about 50 years, he was quietly spoken and with a rather cultured voice. I am sure in earlier life he was a reasonably well-educated man and was probably in good employ.

My neighbour Dave Barnyard used to in a way look after this tramp. When his visit was due Dave would collect items from his colleagues such as cast off clothes, shoes or boots, non-perishable food and we also had a whip round so that we could give him some money. These gifts were graciously received.

About five to six days later the tramp would be on the move, always along the A418 towards Haddenham and Thame; that would be the last we would see of him until the following November.

It would be interesting to have had a talk with him to find if he had any family, what he did in his earlier life, and whether on his travels he followed the same route each year but he was reticent to talk about his earlier years. He was obviously happy with his nomadic existence.

DESTINED FOR HIGH OFFICE, UNTIL.....

When Woman Police Constable Sandra Picket, fresh from the training school arrived at Aylesbury Police Station she caused quite a stir. Very pretty and with a good figure, together with a friendly demeanour, she was an instant hit with the single men and even with a couple of the married sergeants.

One of the sergeants took it upon himself to give her some individual training. Sergeant Jack, whenever the opportunity arose took her out on patrol and on one occasion he said he would show her what was the old fashioned way of carrying out a routine 'stop and search."

It was a Sunday and quiet on the streets of Aylesbury, when they saw a man who did not appear to be a local, the officers checked him out and as he did not give the right reply to questions put to him, he was taken to the police station for further questioning. There it was discovered that he matched a photograph and an article that had been published in the Police Gazette. He was wanted by Bedfordshire Constabulary for a burglary at Dunstable.

He was arrested and later handed over to officers from Dunstable.

That was not the end of the matter, Sergeant Jack submitted a report to the superintendent that WPC Picket, alone on patrol had recognised the man from a photograph she had earlier seen in the Police Gazette, and on her own initiative had arrested the man. The sergeant recommended that the WPC should be commended for her keen observation and initiative. She was duly commended.

She did not deserve a commendation, as on her own confidential admission to me, the sergeant had carried out the questioning and the other enquiries and then put her name to the paperwork; no doubt he was seeking favours from that young and pretty probationary constable.

The Police Gazette, published by the Metropolitan Police and circulated to all police stations, often carried details of wanted persons and other such useful information and it was in this publication that the WPC had allegedly seen the wanted notice.

WPC Picket completed her two years probationary period and then surprisingly, in view of her potential, tendered her resignation. At the same time Sergeant Jack was posted to High Wycombe. I wonder if there was a connection between these two moves!

THE PESKY NUISANCE

During my early days on the beat in Aylesbury I was occasionally pestered by a youth who resided on the Southcourt Estate. He was a gangling lad with a pointy head, sticking out ears, irregular teeth and a spotty face.

He and his little band of followers seemed to get their pleasure in following me and making snide and insulting remarks about me personally and the police generally. He knew how far he could go; never far enough that would allow me to take firm action against him and cautions did not seem to deter him.

Later he bought a motorcycle so now I had the opportunity to give him a bit of hassle. I would occasionally stop him and thoroughly check the machine and then require him to produce his documents at the police station.

He did not wear a helmet so I had another opportunity to reprimand him. (Although the legal requirement to wear a safety helmet whilst riding a motorcycle did not come into force until the 1st June 1973.) Even so my periodical checks did not deter him from his annoying ways.

Then he got himself a girlfriend and that completely changed his attitude towards me, he pointedly avoided me, even crossing to the other side of the road so our paths did not cross.

On one occasion when we did come face to face whilst he was with his girlfriend I took the opportunity to give him payback, I asked,

"Why have you stopped making snide and insulting remarks to me and the police, I miss them?"

He coloured up and quickly walked away without replying.

My nemesis, was involved in a serious accident whilst riding his motorcycle; he suffered major head injuries possibly through not wearing a helmet and unfortunately, was reduced to the state of a cabbage.

A nuisance he may have been but I would not have wished his pestering to stop in this way.

SHEEP (AND COPPER) DIPPING

One of the police duties in those early days of my service was to supervise sheep dipping. Once or twice a year farmers were required to dip all their sheep in a foul smelling chemical to kill off parasites. It was the constable's job to count the sheep being dipped and to ensure they were fully immersed in the liquid.

Sergeant Jim Mellows told me one morning that I had to go to Quainton Farm to supervise sheep dipping so off I went.

Can you imagine it, a brand new shiny constable, with highly polished boots, sharply creased tunic and trousers, helmet on straight and wearing white gloves, mounted on my very clean new Raleigh cycle, riding down the Bicester Road, Aylesbury? Proudly I rode down that road as I was on a very important mission, sheep dipping.

Alas, I misjudged how long it would take to cycle to Quainton and was late arriving at the farm to be met by an irate farmer as I had kept him and his men waiting. He then brusquely said

"Follow me."

I did so and he took me across the farmyard through ankle deep slurry and cow muck, my immaculately polished Doc Martins were soon covered, inside and out, as were the bottoms of my trousers. Now I was not happy.

The farmer sensing I was new to the job suggested that I should stand at the end of the concrete ramp to best supervise the operation and to ensure the dipping task was carried out properly and the sheep counted.

Pocket book and pencil at the ready I was geared up to count and tick every sheep as they came out of the dip.

The sheep were brought into a holding pen, then one at a time the first man shepherded the first one out, the second man chivvied it along a wicker fenced channel and then pushed or literally threw it into a pit filled with the odious fluid. The third man standing on a raised platform beside the pit ensured they were completely dipped by pushing their heads under with a long forked stick. The sheep, once well dipped, was then allowed to struggle up the ramp and out into the field.

The first sheep went in with an almighty splash, it was well and truly dipped, then it came up the ramp towards me, paused, gave itself a vigorous shake and you guessed it, I was completely sprayed from head to toe with the foul smelling liquid.

The farmer and his farmhands split their sides with laughter. They were highly amused and had a job keeping the big grins off their faces. They knew what was going to happen but the stupid constable didn't. That was, no doubt the farmer's revenge for my tardy arrival. And to think I was the son of a farmer!

I rapidly moved to another position.

After the dipping was over the farmer was more kind to me. To sign off the paperwork we went back to the farmhouse via the orchard I then realised he had earlier deliberately walked me through the muddy farmyard.

Later that day, in sharp contrast to that once shiny new constable, I rode back up the Bicester Road covered in muck and smelling of that foul liquid. I was not so proud and important now, but a whole lot wiser.

ALL TIED UP

It was a hot summer afternoon so I was standing in the shade of an empty shop doorway in the High Street, opposite the Vale recreation ground, when I saw something rather odd.

A portly man, aged between 50 to 60 years old, stopped and untied his left bootlace. He then stopped a pretty young lady in a summery dress and appeared to ask her to tie up his lace, she did so and then she walked off.

A few minutes later the man untied his bootlace again, and stopped another young lady who bent down to tie it up for him, and then she walked off. When he undid his lace for the third time the penny dropped. As these helpful ladies were bending over to tie the lace of his boot he was looking down their blouses and getting a good eyeful of their 'attributes'.

Now I had heard about men looking up ladies skirts as they go up the stairs or maybe a ladder but not of men ogling ladies chests as they bent down to help old men with their laces.

I approached the man and told him I knew what he was up to and I was taking him down to the station, but did not arrest him as quite frankly I had no idea what crime he may have committed.

At the station Inspector Cameron listened to the evidence, perused some law books and came to the conclusion that the man had been doing a bit of voyeurism, but we could not find any appropriate legislation under which we could charge him.

By way of explanation the man said that the first lady had tied the lace too tightly so he had undone them, and the second lady tied it too loosely and this is why he again untied it. We were not convinced.

The man was not charged but he left the police station with his ears ringing from the tongue-lashing he received from the inspector.

LADY DRIVERS

We all know that many men believe the opposite sex are inferior drivers compared to male drivers, so it must be true.

It started to snow about 9am and it soon lay four to five inches thick on the roads, not the weather to be out for a drive.

About midday a passing motorist stopped in Buckingham Street and told me that there had been an accident at Waddesdon crossroads and he thought a couple of drivers had been injured. I telephoned the station and Sergeant Jim told me that he would call an ambulance and I should make my way to the scene.

I stopped the first car that came along and then realised it was being driven by a lady, but this was not the time to be picky. I asked her to take me to Waddesdon. She told me she was travelling from London to Coventry so it was on her way.

Now that lady driver drove like an expert, she drove calmly and competently and coped with all the skids and slides as if it was second nature to her. To be that capable to drive so confidently I believe she must have spent some driving time in Canada or Scandinavia.

We arrived safely at Waddesdon crossroads just after the ambulance had loaded up the two male drivers. After thanking the lady driver for the lift, with the help of a couple of other motorists we moved the two damaged cars off the road.

I dealt with the accident, filled out the accident report and then hitched a lift back to Aylesbury in a lorry.

At the Royal Bucks Hospital I was pleased to see that

the two male drivers were not seriously injured and after taking short statements and completing the accident form TA1 I resumed my patrol.

Not all women drivers are incompetent and since this little episode I have been careful not to criticise a lady's driving, especially my wife's.

COPPERS AND SMARTNESS

Smartness was a quality I learnt in the army and this was carried forward into my police service. All police officers were expected to be smart in appearance and proper in their manner and when I joined the police force in 1955 this was the norm.

How times have changed. In my hometown of Abingdon I recently saw a person approaching me in the precinct, in uniform and wearing a fluorescent jacket. He was not wearing any headgear or tie, and as he got nearer, I realised I had no idea who he was. The only clue was the amount of gear he was carrying. I noted his shoes were reasonably clean but bereft of a shine; his combat trousers were crumpled and had no visage of a crease.

I wondered, was he a police constable, a special

constable, a PCSO (Police Community Support Officer), a traffic warden, council official, or even an employee of one of the public utilities? No, as he passed I noted he had the word 'Police' printed on the back of the fluorescent jacket. This was the only indication of his employ.

What a change in appearance from when I was a young constable and in my view not for the better. I was under the impression that a police constable wore a distinctive uniform so that he was instantly recognisable.

In 2009, my former force, The Thames Valley Police, along with several other forces, decided to do away with helmets and officers were issued with flat caps and/or baseball caps. I hope I do not see officers wearing baseball caps back to front, or even sideways, now that would be the limit.

THE NIGHT I CLOSED THE POLICE STATION

It must have been during the summer as it was a warm night when I was on reserve duty at Aylesbury police station. Sergeant Jim went off duty at 2am and the only other constable on duty was on the town centre patrol.

Just after 3am the emergency call came through from the owner of an off-licence store at the bottom of Aylesbury High Street. In a whispered voice the owner, who lived above the store, told me he could hear someone moving about in the shop below.

I rang Headquarters but no patrol car was available, the town centre constable had just made his 3am conference point so would not be contactable for another forty minutes. I had to make a decision as to the best course of action.

I closed the station, got on my cycle and made haste to the off-licence. As I approached I saw a man run out of the store, cross the High Street and make his way to the toilets in the Vale Recreation Ground.

Leaving my bike with the store owner I ran to the toilets, then another problem arose, male or female toilet first, working on instinct I went into the men's, slammed open both cubicles – the place was empty. As I ran out I saw the miscreant running across the recreation ground, he must have been in the ladies. I gave chase but the farther away we got from the High Street lights the harder it was to see him. After running around for some time I must admit I lost him.

Returning to the liquor store I took details of the

burglary from the owner collected my bike and returned to the station. There I made up the crime report and put an entry in the occurrence book.

At 6am, looking forward to my bed, the early turn sergeant told me to hold on as he had called out the inspector and the detective inspector who may wish to talk to me.

When the two senior officers arrived they interviewed me, well a better term would be interrogated me for over an hour while a constable took it all down in shorthand. I then had to sign a multi-page typed statement. The way those senior officers interrogated me I felt like I was the one who had committed the burglary.

I wonder what their attitude would have been if I had not done anything until the town centre constable was contactable at 4am. I would probably have been charged with neglect of duty. I know the owner of the off-licence store would not have been happy.

From experience of what police life was like in those days I can say that in all probability no other telephone calls would have been made, or persons would have visited the police station in the thirty minutes or so I was away from the station during the early hours of the morning.

I was not disciplined so I can only assume the

superintendent considered my actions that night to be reasonable and probably for the best.

It is interesting to note that over the past few years hundreds of police stations in small towns throughout the country are closed between 5pm and 9am and many more have been completely closed for good. How times have changed.

CHIMNEY FIRES AND PROCESS CHASERS

In the 1950's and before central heating was the norm; chimney fires were a frequent occurrence and police constables always made their way to the scene of these incidents.

After the Fire Brigade had done their work the constable would then report 'for summons' the owner for, 'being the occupier of a dwelling house the chimney of which accidentally caught fire', contrary to the Town Police Clauses Act of 1847. The penalty was a 10/- fine. (Fifty pence today).

When I joined, the Police and Fire Brigade shared the same radio frequency so we knew what each other were doing; we could listen in to the Fire Brigade calls so were aware of the location of a chimney fire.

When this Act was formulated no doubt there were more thatched houses about and sparks from a chimney fire could have a devastating effect so the Act made sense. However, on the modern estate with tiled roofs there was not so much danger from a chimney fire.

On reflection, reporting the occupier for allowing his chimney to catch fire in the 1950's was a waste of time but it did add to the monthly tally of offences reported by the constable.

During my time on the beat I had no knowledge of any occupier being summoned; all these offences were dealt with by way of caution.

Occasionally new recruits would get themselves into a bit of bother over these offences. I have known quite a few young constables that would follow the fire engine to a chimney fire in villages just outside Aylesbury such as Bierton and Stone, then report the occupier for the offence of allowing their chimney to catch fire but on return to the station, and submitting their process report, they would be castigated by the sergeant – the Town Police Clauses Act as the name implies only applied in designated towns!

A LADY IN DISTRESS

I was on office duty when a distressed lady called in. She complained that as she was walking along a lane, car had drawn up beside her; the driver got out, opened his mac, and exposed himself to her.

As tactful as possible, I asked her, "Did he have an erection?" She replied, "No, it was a Ford Cortina."

Well, what could I say to that, we were not taught at the Training College how to deal with that sort of conversation.

ARE YOU A PUBLIC OR PRIVATE SERVANT?

One afternoon I was with Sergeant Jim Mellows in Aylesbury Market Square when a Rolls Royce car stopped on the other side of the square and the driver beckoned us over, I was about to go and see what he wanted when Jim said

"Stay."

I stayed. Then I recognised the driver as a well-known actor and comedian, Donald Williams. (Not his real name).

Despite his continued gesticulating we stood firm and eventually the actor got out of the car, came across the Market Square and looking somewhat angry said to us,

"Why didn't you come when I beckoned, I remind you, you are public servants."

Jim said,

"That is correct sir, but we are not your private servant, how can we help you?"

That put him in his place.

A DRINK PLEASE - REFUSED

On another occasion I again met up with the actor Donald Williams. He used to own his own light plane and when he buzzed his home somewhere near Whitchurch this caused a number of complaints from the residents, the upshot was that he was summoned for the offence of low flying over residential districts.

He elected trial and the case came up before the judge at the Assize Court in Aylesbury.

In those early days and prior to the opening of the Assize Courts, the judges used to go to the church for prayers – I suppose they prayed they would make the right decisions at the upcoming trials. Then after the church service the Judge, with the Lord Lieutenant, the County Sheriff, the Mayor, the Chief Constable and other court dignitaries, all in their fineries, would walk in a slow procession to the court building escorted by constables carrying pikes.

On the first day of the trial of Mr Donald Williams I was one of the court officers and as the norm stood near the court door holding a seven-foot pike, no, not a fish but one of those ceremonial things.

During a period when the Judge and Counsel had retired for a short discussion, Donald Williams, from the dock beckoned me; I had more important duties to perform so I ignored him.

Eventually, his solicitor came to me and said somewhat irately that his client wanted me to get him a glass of water and would I get it pronto. I told him to speak to the usher. No way was I going to act as lackey to someone who was in the dock for a serious offence no matter how famous he may have been. I was following Sergeant Jim Mellows' correct example.

MY FIRST PROPER DRIVE IN A POLICE CAR

My first chance to drive a police car any distance was after I had been in the police for a couple of years. A girl had escaped from a Young Woman's Institution, made her way to Aylesbury where she was caught stealing from a shop.

At the Magistrate's Court she was sentenced to detention at the Y.W.I. at Barry Island, South Wales. A woman police constable and I were instructed to take her there.

Did I dream it or did I think the sergeant really had told me to take her to Bali Island? A trip to Indonesia would have been very nice.

We were not provided with refreshments, money or even a map, I had not been to Wales before, I had no idea where Barry Island was, I had not even heard of the place.

We set off from Aylesbury about 2pm and knowing the institute would probably be shut down by 6pm we made rapid progress in the police station's Austin A40.

Eventually, we found Barry Island but could not find the Institute but by a stroke of good luck and by asking the right person we eventually arrived at the Institute. It was shut.

We had not travelled all that way to be turned back. Eventually, after a lot of banging on the door we attracted the attention of a member of staff and reluctantly they accepted the young girl.

Now we had the long journey back to Aylesbury. It was then approaching midnight and the WPC and I had been on continuous duty since 9am.

Fortunately the weather was fine and dry, even so we were so tired that at 3am we stopped at an all night transport café on the A40 east of Cheltenham to get something to eat and drink.

Police officers just did not do that in those days and it caused some raised eyebrows from the truckers – male and female police constables in uniform in the middle of the night, a long way from habitation doing something unusual, eating in a public place, but by then we were passed caring.

We arrived back at Aylesbury Police Station about 4:30am and were sent off duty to get a well-earned rest. We had been on duty for nineteen and a half hours with only a short break – and we did not get paid overtime or any expenses.

A MEETING WITH A BULL

Paddy Murnane, an Irishman, was one of the sergeants at Aylesbury during my early years there. Unlike the other sergeants he was not a strict disciplinarian, more like a father figure and easy to work with.

I recall that during night duty and when it was quiet he would call in the constables off their beats and give us talks on geography, politics, history, as well as police matters. He was well versed in all matters intellectual. These interludes made a pleasant change from pounding the beat.

Ken was a former sailor, he was a good copper but prone at times to be arrogant and abrasive. When Sergeant Paddy told me one morning to accompany Ken on a delicate enquiry at a farm near Stoke Mandeville, I was prepared for, well if not fireworks then a little bit of a fracas. Perhaps Sergeant Paddy thought I would have a calming influence on Ken.

Ken wanted to interview a man who lived on the farm about a rather delicate matter and when we arrived there the farmer told Ken the man he wanted to see was in a caravan the other side of a field and about 300 yards from the farmhouse. A field that contained a large herd of cattle.

Ken started off towards the field gate then the farmer cautioned him,

"Don't go through the field."

Ken in his usual brusque manner turned and producing his warrant card he flashed it to the farmer and said,

"You see this, this warrant card is the authority of the police and I can go anywhere I wish – any time – on any land – do I make myself clear?"

And with that somewhat rude comment Ken was off, he climbed over the gate and was about 100 yards into the field when we saw him turned round and run back towards the gate. Ken had seen that amongst the herd of cattle there was the most enormous bull who must have thought Ken was going to harm its harem, and had started to advance towards Ken, hence the rapid retreat.

Ken ran as fast as he could and as he got near the gate, with the bull some fifty yards behind, the farmer ran to the gate and called out at the top of his lungs,

"Your warrant card, show the bull your police authority."

Ken just made it over the gate and to safety but he was not amused.

The farmer had a point, if Ken had cared to listen to him for a moment he would have been told not to go into the field because of the bull.

Perhaps Ken did not know that old rustic's saying, "The farmer allows walkers to cross the field for free, but the bull charges!!"

Taking a roundabout way to the caravan Ken concluded his enquiry but on the way back to the station he was unusually quiet.

Whilst Ken was making his enquiries I chatted with the farmer, as a farmer's son I was interested in all things agricultural.

We were discussing his livestock and how he kept them; he told me he had three fields, sheep, cows and summer sheep and cows. He must have noticed my bemused look, in any event I asked,

"What are summer sheep and cows?"

He explained,

"Over there is a field of cows, over there is a field of sheep and in that field there, some are sheep and some are cows."

The farmer was so po-faced I was not sure if he was joking or if it was a figure of speech.

THE VESPA SCOOTER

After a couple of years in the police I was able to afford to buy a form of motorised transport, a Vespa scooter, for £40. At last, my wife and I were going upmarket and we were truly mobile.

Unfortunately, it was gutless and with a pillion passenger it could hardly manage 35 mph. I had to get something more suitable so I advertised it for sale in the local paper for £40. I would be prepared to take £35 or at a push go down to £30.

A few days later there was a knock on the door (no telephones in those days) and there was a young man who wanted to see the scooter. I took him through the house to the back garden where he looked at my gleaming scooter, a bit of hard polishing had worked wonders as far as looks were concerned.

He asked for a test ride, I agreed as long as he did not leave the private gravel drive at the back of the house, as he was not insured.

After a wobbly start he was away, up to the end of the drive, onto the public roadway and away into the distance.

I was decidedly unhappy; I had told him that he

would not be insured. What should I do when he came back, should I report him for riding the bike without insurance and jeopardise the chance of a sale.

If I did take him to court he may say I had given him permission to go on the public roads and then I would be in trouble for permitting the scooter to be used without insurance.

Then another thought hit me, what if he did not come back at all, had he stolen my scooter?

That would be a real embarrassment. How would I explain to my colleagues at the police station that I had allowed someone who was uninsured to steal my scooter?

Ten to fifteen minutes later I was relieved to hear the stutter of that two-stroke engine as it came back up the road.

As I walked towards the end of the drive, the young man turned in from the road, skidded on the gravel, and crashed into the side of a house. I ran and picked up the scooter – he could pick himself up. I saw that one side of the scooter was quite badly damaged.

The young man, who suffered minor abrasions, on seeing the damage to the Vespa caused, said,

"I think I had better buy it."

He handed over the money and as I looked at those

forty new banknotes I had a touch of amnesia and totally forgot about his uninsured ride!

THE LOCAL LADY OF EASY VIRTUE

About 150 yards from our house there was the corner shop, run by a nice married couple that lived in the flat above the shop. Above the shop extension at the rear was an annex in which their daughter lived.

The daughter had a reputation of being a girl of easy virtue, she seemed to have a continual stream of boyfriends, surprising as she was not very attractive and was somewhat overweight. Her oversized bosom being counterbalanced by her oversized rear, but despite this she had a long term boy-friend who was of a violent nature and their domestic disputes were a constant bother to me.

I was living at 83 Stoke Road from October 1955 until we moved into a new house in March 1959 and during that time at least once every three months I had that girl, or one of her parents, in a state of distress knocking at my door because the boyfriend had become violent.

As often happens, by the time police were called the

assailant had turned contrite, promised on his grannies life he would not be violent again so he was forgiven by the poor deluded girl.

Despite the regular calls I received on none of those occasions would the silly girl make a statement of complaint!

I was glad to move, not only into a newly built and warm and lovely house, but to get away from this troublesome couple. Oh, the penalties of being a local bobby.

TONY IS IN TROUBLE

Tony joined the police about six months after I had joined. He was a reasonably good policeman although a bit lazy at times. Due to his laziness he did get in a bit of bother in court when giving evidence about an accident we had both attended.

Tony and I arrived at the scene of the accident on the A418 road at Dinton, between the towns of Aylesbury and Thame. A motorist had tried to overtake another car just before a bend and crashed into a car coming from the opposite direction. The outcome was the overtaking driver was summoned for dangerous or careless driving.

At the scene I had asked Tony, the constable dealing with the accident, if he wanted help in taking measurements but despite my advice that measurements would be an essential part of his evidence against the offending driver, he declined the offer stating he was good at estimating distances.

When the case came up at the Aylesbury Magistrate's Court the offending driver pleaded not guilty. At issue was how far away the offending driver was from the bend when he commenced the overtaking move.

Tony had estimated it at less than thirty yards but the driver disagreed. This is where Tony's evidence fell down.

The collision had left score marks at the point of impact and the defence solicitor's clerk, with the driver had accurately measured from those marks to the bend and it was in excess of 60 yards, twice Tony's estimate.

The Defence Solicitor, an Aylesbury man, was a very fair and well respected person who as a general rule would not attack the policeman's evidence but in this case he knew the officer was wrong, seriously wrong.

The more Tony was questioned the more flustered he became. As I was on court duty that day it was embarrassing for me at the back of the court to see him squirming so much. I was pleased that I was not called to give evidence as I also knew Tony was in the wrong.

The magistrates determined the case 'not proven'. Tony left the court with egg on his face, I am sure he learnt a lesson from this episode.

It is of paramount importance that evidence presented to a court is accurate and complete as Tony found to his embarrassment, his evidence was just not accurate enough.

I have often been asked whether giving evidence in court is a nerve wracking or stressful experience and the answer it an emphatic "yes".

I concede that despite my many years of experience even towards the end of my service I still got butterflies in my stomach as I approached the witness box.

It is the knowledge that questions may be asked to which I did not have the appropriate answer or I had made a monumental error in some way.

Despite initial nerves when I entered the witness box my abiding strength was always the same, that the evidence I was about to give to the court would be the truth, the whole truth and nothing but the truth.

From that position I would not be moved and that

was a great comfort and morale booster.

A BIT OF A PUNCH-UP.

I have only been assaulted twice in my thirty years with the police, which meant I have been either fortunate or very diplomatic.

The first occasion was about 4:30am in Cambridge Street, Aylesbury. This is a one-way street and I saw a van travelling along it in the wrong direction and then stop outside a shop. I stepped out of a doorway and confronted the driver who I knew as a former bad boy, a rogue and stallholder, and now a greengrocer who had recently purchased the shop. I recall he was driving a brand new Ford Transit van, the first one I had seen.

I asked him for his documents that he produced. I recorded the details in my pocket book and handed them back to him, walked to the front of the van to note the registration number, when totally unexpectedly, he hit me on the side of the head with a haymaker, knocking me to the ground.

Fortunately for me, as I struggled to get up and pick up my pocket book and pencil and put my helmet back on, Sergeant Mitchell who was driving the police van down Cambridge Street had witnessed the assault and before I realised what had happened the driver had been arrested, handcuffed and bundled into the back of the Police van.

The man was subsequently charged and at Aylesbury Magistrate's Court he came up before the Chairman of the Bench, Lady Rothschild. Now Lady Rothschild did not like to hear about constables being assaulted and she gave him a good talking to. I remember she always referred to police officers as 'MY' officers.

He was convicted for assaulting a police constable and fined. Oh, I almost forget, he was also convicted of travelling down a one-way street the wrong way.

IT'S SNOW JOKE

The second occasion was not so much as an assault on me but a free for all in a snowdrift. I was then a member of the Traffic Department and teamed up with Mel Lipscombe.

Mel and I were on nights, and it was our normal procedure in those days, halfway through our shift, to call into the Headquarters control room where we usually dined with the switchboard operators, a constable and a civilian.

The civilian was a very good cook. We all contributed to the ingredients that he purchased and he cooked us a first class meal.

It was about 1am, it had been snowing and about four inches was lying on the road and it was drifting. Not the night to be out driving and the early part of the night had been very quiet.

Then there was a telephone call from a public house on the outskirts of Wendover, which was about seven miles away.

Apparently Martin, a police constable himself, had woken the publican up. He asked the landlord to call the police as his car was stuck in a snowdrift and he needed help.

Martin was a married man with two children and also my neighbour. He was off duty and I knew he had been out drinking or womanising, or both as this was his usual Saturday night practice. I did not get on with him, did not like the way he conducted his social life and my first inclination was to ignore his call for help.

But, he was a colleague so we turned out and started off for Wendover.

Apparently, whilst we were making our way through the thick snow things were happening at the scene. Martin had seen and flagged down a Land Rover and asked the two occupants to give him a tow out of the snowdrift.

They offered to do so providing he paid them ten bob (50 pence in today's money). Martin, in his usual charming way swore at them using quite a large number of choice words so the two men drove off leaving him there.

After travelling for a short distance the two men had different thoughts and full of indignation for being sworn at, returned to where Martin was, his car still stuck in the snowdrift, and commenced to beat him up.

When we arrived the men were still thumping him and Martin was by then badly injured and defenceless.

Mel and I waded into the two men with the intention of affecting their arrest. Foolishly, I took on the bigger man and during the struggle took quite a few punches. I recall at one time I was on top of the man in a snowdrift trying to twist his arm up his back and put handcuffs on him and their dog jumped onto my back and was trying to bite me. Fortunately, I was wearing my greatcoat so the dog was not successful.

Eventually the two men were subdued, arrested,

handcuffed and taken into custody. Meanwhile Martin was taken to hospital, he had been seriously injured.

Both men were convicted of assault at the Quarter Sessions and fined £50 each, a goodly sum in those days. Shortly after Martin left the police on retirement and I was relieved, he was not a good officer. I did not go to his farewell party.

THE EXTRA SPECIAL CONSTABLE

Special Constable Ron lived a couple of streets away from our house in Priory Crescent. He was reasonably good at the job, he was also very good with the ladies and we saw him about with, so it seemed, a different girl every day of the week.

A single man, dapper in appearance and with a charming manner, he attracted girls like bees are attracted to a honey pot.

One day I jokingly commented to him that he appeared to have so many girlfriends that it would seem he had a concubine (I really meant to say a harem) he replied,

"The secret is you have to treat concubines like you

would treat Woodbines, take just one a day and you will enjoy them more and you will live much longer."

I had to take his word for it as my wife would not let me have either a concubine or a harem, and I did not smoke.

THE GRAND OLD LADY OF WADDESDON

A frequent visitor to Aylesbury Police Station was an elderly lady from Waddesdon. She had problems with aliens from space paying periodic and unwelcome visits to her house.

On average every three months she would call in and ask the police to take action to prevent these visits.

I do not know which constable found a cure to her problem but it was a bit of the lore at Aylesbury Police Station that on her request for help the reserve constable would make just one telephone call, then she would be untroubled for the next three months or so.

At Wescott, a few miles north of Waddesdon, there was then the Government Rocket Research Establishment and the reserve constable would make a pretend telephone call to this establishment requesting them to throw an electronic screen around the lady's house thereby preventing the aliens getting through. It worked.

Her request was treated with due respect and attention and occasionally she even asked the police to contact the Government Rocket Research Establishment on her behalf.

I was on reserve duty one day when she called in with her usual complaint and by making that bogus telephone call her fears about aliens were allayed for a few more months. She then said to me,

"You are a very kind man, bless you, you will go to heaven." (As well as suffering from alien visitors she was a very religious lady.)

I said, "I will not be going to heaven."

To which she retorted,

"Why ever not, you are a God fearing man."

To which I replied for some stupid reason,

"I would not like to go up there. I do not have a head for heights."

She walked out of the police station shaking her head.

My reply to her was as daft as her request had been to

me.

Despite her obvious mental problem she was a gracious and lovely lady.

THE SCOUSE SCAFFOLDERS

In the 1950's Aylesbury was undergoing a lot of building work and a number of scaffolders had been drafted in from the Liverpool area to help in this work.

About 10:15pm one evening I was called to a disturbance in a public house in Back Buckingham Street. I was the only constable on duty in the town centre and knowing the reputation of these hard drinking northerners it was with some trepidation that I made my way to the pub.

When I arrived there I found the dispute was between the landlord and four scaffolders. The landlord had told them to leave but they refused and wanted more drinks.

In my diplomatic manner I persuaded the scaffolders to leave having told them I knew a better pub where they would be more than welcome.

Once outside the public house I pointed out to them that all the pubs would be closed by 10:30pm and 'time up' would be called within ten minutes so it was not worth their bother to continue their pub crawl. The scaffolders saw the sense in this suggestion and agreed to return to their lodgings.

I watched as they walked away, then after about 100 yards they stopped, turned and one came back towards me, my first thought was - more trouble - but he came up to me and said he wanted to shake my hand as it was the first time a policeman had got either him or his mates out of a pub without whacking them with a night stick.

Apparently, it was the normal practice for constables in Merseyside to carry a truncheon during the day but at night they carried a longer truncheon called a nightstick and the officers up north did not hesitate to use them when the opportunity arose.

It seemed us southerners were a bit more laid back and relied more on tact than brute force.

ROBIN OR BATMAN!

Occasionally, due to the shortage of constables we had to work ARD's - Additional Rest Days. I do not know why they were called ARD's, as they certainly were not rest days. These were worked rest days and constables were paid overtime so the money was very welcome. It did however mean working with another shift.

On one of these working rest days I was with the night shift that had a constable who I will call Robin Batman. An ex-university man he was obviously well educated. He was about 6' 4" tall, gangly and he walked as if his legs were not properly connected to his hips.

On the night in question I was on reserve duty when the front door of the police station burst open and a man in a state of distress entered and demanded to see the sergeant. I did not have to call the sergeant as he could hear the commotion from his office. The motorist had a complaint about one of the constables.

In those days after midnight every person on foot, cycling or in a motor vehicle was stopped by police, checked and details recorded by the beat constables.

Constables were issued with torches that had red and green flaps and if it were necessary to stop a motor vehicle during the hours of darkness the torch with red flap in place would be swung slowly back and forth indicating the driver to stop.

On this occasion in Aylesbury Market Square, the reason for the irate motorist making the complaint was that Constable Robin Batman did not bother with his torch; he leapt out of a doorway in front of this motorist waving his arms about.

Can you imagine this huge gangling black being, with cape flapping about suddenly and unexpectedly leaping in front of you? As the motorist complained, it was like being confronted by a huge black bat. He said that his heart was beating so fast he thought he was going to have a heart attack.

After the motorist had calmed down and sent on his way, the constable was duly 'educated' by Sergeant Jim.

I recall another incident involving this constable; he was working an ARD and on this occasion with my 2pm to 10pm shift. He was patrolling the High Street and Market Square beat.

About 8pm we received a telephone call from a member of the public that the traffic lights at the top of the High Street were no longer working. These lights are at the junction of the High Street, Market Square, Kingsbury Square, Cambridge Street and Back Buckingham Street, so they could be very busy.

Collecting the spare traffic light keys, Sergeant Jim Mellows and I went out to see what was wrong. At the traffic lights we met up with Constable Robin Batman, he told us that as the traffic was reasonably light he had switched off the traffic lights to save electricity!

Needless to say Sergeant Jim gave him some more, very forceful, on the spot education.

To sum up, Robin Batman was very highly educated but was entirely bereft of common sense - and he lasted less than nine months in the police.

FIRST AID AND A HELPFUL LADY

In the late 1950's I was a member of the Buckinghamshire Constabulary First Aid Team and we used to compete in regional and national first aid competitions against other police forces, the Ambulance Service, Fire Brigade, St John's Ambulance, the Army and Royal Air Force. These events were arranged by the Casualty Union and entailed quite a lot of training and travelling.

Our instructor was a fifty year old male ex-ambulance driver aided by a 30ish year old single lady who acted as the 'patient.'

She was quite an attractive and petite young lady who appeared to like being manhandled by us constables who had to check out her body for broken bones, etc, particularly those in the thigh area.

She also liked us to give her artificial respiration, be it mouth to mouth or chest depressions. She almost purred with delight during these training sessions. Despite these distractions we were a good, well-disciplined team as our many certificates could testify.

As time went by I learnt that this young lady had been inviting a couple of our team members to her home in the Bicester Road, Aylesbury for 'private tuition.' I am sure this tuition included a lot of 'in depth' examinations.

When she invited me to engage in a bit of private tuition I declined.

As a newly married young man I did not want any complications of that nature in my life. One woman was enough; two women would be like having a double bout of flu.

A move to Bletchley in 1966 brought to an end my

involvement with the Aylesbury First Aid Team and that enticing young lady.

TRAFFIC - AYLESBURY

In June 1960 I was transferred to the Traffic Department much to my delight, as it was one of my ambitions to drive a traffic patrol car. In those days the Buckinghamshire Constabulary used Riley Pathfinders and Jaguar 2.4's. The Riley's were being phased out so my experience with them was limited, not that it mattered as the Jaguar was a far superior car. My ambition was being realised.

As part of my training I had to attend a traffic patrol course at Essex Police Headquarters, Chelmsford. This was an intensive high-speed course requiring a high degree of driving skill.

I had learnt to drive in a small tank (a Bren Gun Carrier) whilst in the army, passed my driving test in a Bedford three ton army lorry, had ridden motorcycles in competitions and then rallied cars for a number of years so I had an all-round background in motor vehicles.

I do not know if this was of benefit on the course but

I did eventually obtain a first class driving qualification with 89/100.

THE RILEY PATHFINDER

One of the driving standards we had to strive for on the driving course was smoothness, no jerky gear-change, sharp acceleration or braking, no sudden swerving, in other words the car had to flow swiftly along. The instructor drummed into us the words 'passenger consideration'.

Some months after I joined the Traffic Department and had completed the driving course, a request was received from the Metropolitan Police for a witness to be collected from Winslow and transported to Denham where he would be transferred to a Metropolitan police car for onward transportation.

Apparently the witness was urgently required at the Old Bailey in London in relation to a murder trial and the request came from the Presiding Judge.

I picked up the witness at Winslow in one of the Riley Pathfinders and on the way he commented that the car had a very smooth automatic gearbox as he could not feel or hear the car changing gear. I advised him that the car had a manual gearbox and I had changed gear many times during the journey.

He looked flummoxed until I told him the gear lever was on the right side of the car, between the driver's seat and the door.

I could have left him in ignorance but on the other hand I did pride myself in being a smooth driver, thanks to that driving course.

ROMAN ROADS

THEY DON'T LIKE IT UP 'EM MR MANNERING

Generally Roman roads in our country are fairly straight. Essex and the surrounding counties have their share of Roman roads, some of them were not always that straight, they seemed to zig zag around a bit.

Our instructor told us, his pupils that the reason the roads in this area were bendier than other Roman roads was because of the prevailing winds off the North Sea.

He then said that those Roman road workers did not like the cold north-east wind blowing up their togas so, as far as possible, they worked with the wind side-on and if the wind changed direction so did they, hence the winding roads.

As Corporal Jones would say, "They don't like it up 'em Mr Mannering."

I reckon this was a lot of East Anglian nonsense.

COPPERS WITH COPPERS TO SPARE

When I joined the police in 1955 we were paid our wages on the Friday and we always looked forward to that little envelope with a few pounds in it.

In the early 1960's the Buckinghamshire Constabulary decided to go modern and pay the money direct into the police constable's bank.

Now my crewmate Mel, he was very 'anti' this, protested that he did not have a bank account and he had no intention of opening one. No way was the bank going to have his money, he had earned it and he would keep it to himself.

He was not the only copper who took this attitude and there was quite a lot of opposition to this new way of paying our wages; however the powers-that-be prevailed.

Reluctantly Mel opened a bank account. He tried to find any and every reason to criticise this new payment system and as his crewmate I had to endure his constant complaining.

About six months later Mel told me he liked the new payment system as for the first time in his life he had spare money in the bank account, about £50.

Apparently, when it was cash in hand he spent it as he got it but when he had to draw it out of the bank he drew just enough to get by on, thereby building up a healthy balance.

Perhaps our paymasters new best after all. At least the constant complaining stopped.

THE DEAF MUTE

When I joined the Traffic Department I was teamed up with Mel. It was a nice change after five years pounding the beat to drive around in a shiny black Jaguar patrol car.

Mel, an ex-paratrooper, was ten years more senior to me in police service so he was a good man to be teamed up with.

During their probationary period constables served a two-week attachment to the CID and then two weeks with the Traffic Department. One such probationer called Terry was on his traffic attachment with Mel and me.

Mel, with fifteen years' service and I with five, were experienced coppers and we decided we would show that young, 'green behind the ears' sprog a few tricks during the upcoming two weeks.

We were called to a disturbance in Kingsbury Square, Aylesbury where several men, kicked out of a pub, were involved in a drunken brawl and throwing punches at each other.

We drove up with the blue light flashing and bell ringing (no sirens in those days). We did not sound the bell to hasten our way to the incident but to let the troublemakers know we were on our way. It had the desired effect. On hearing the bell most of those troublesome people outside the pub faded into the background and on our arrival we only had three men to deal with.

Mel, Terry and I got out of the patrol car and walked up to the three remaining men who were still showing signs of aggression. Mel, in his usual calm 'George Dixon way' said, "Evening all". After calming down the men we soon worked out who the ringleader was and when we tried to speak to him he kept touching his ears and mouth, indicating he was a deaf mute.

I noted that our aide Terry had vanished. My first thought was that he would not appear to be much help when there was a bit of trouble.

As Mel and I tried to communicate with the ringleader, hoping he could lip read or understand our hand signals, Terry returned from behind the pub with two metal dustbin lids. He crept up behind the deaf mute and clapped them together causing an almighty crash, a clatter that resounded round and round the square.

Startled, the deaf mute I am sure jumped two feet into the air and then let out a string of expletives that I could not commit to paper.

The supposed deaf mute was no longer deaf or dumb; he had been cured of his twin afflictions by that young sprog's initiative. The man then admitted it was a try-on.

The supposedly deaf mute and the two other men were duly cautioned and sent on their way.

That evening the young constable Terry had shown us, two experienced officers, one of his own tricks.

Later in his service Terry was promoted to detective sergeant. He was a bright spark; there was no doubt about it.

FAMOUS PEOPLE

Mel and I were on our way from Buckingham to Aylesbury when we stopped in the town of Whitchurch to get some sausage rolls for lunch.

As we came out of the shop a couple of tourists stopped us seeking some information about the locality and its people.

In the 1950's and 60's, before Tourist Information Centres and Citizen Advice Bureaus were thought of, it was usually the local copper who was the most reliable source of local information. Any copper worth his salt would know all about the famous and important buildings, its industry and its people.

We, well actually Mel, who was a lot more knowledgeable then I had answered several of their questions then one of them then asked,

"Have any famous people been born in Whitchurch?"

To which Mel, pan-faced replied,

"No, only babies."

They wandered away shaking their heads in bewilderment. I do not believe Mel realised what consternation he had caused.

ROGUES AND RAILWAYS

It was during the summer and on a very hot day when a call came through that a couple of teenagers were thought to be placing objects on the railway line north of Aylesbury.

Mel and I, appreciating the seriousness of the situation, made haste to the location, there we saw two teenagers in a field adjacent to the railway line, no doubt the culprits.

I got out of the patrol car and made my way towards them. Mel chose to stay in the car. When I was about 50 yards away the two lads made a dash for it, I set off in pursuit. Although fairly fit I did not have the stamina of those two young ones but I kept them in sight as I chased them across one field through a hedge and into another field.

I saw ahead and towards where they were heading a large, high and thick hedge, had I got them trapped. No, there was a small gap, I headed for it hoping to cut them off but they must have seen it at the same time and they reached it about 150 yards ahead of me. If they split on reaching the gap which one should I chase?

At the point of exhaustion, hot and sweaty, I arrived at the gap, went through to see the two lads, handcuffed, sitting in the back of the police car with Mel sitting in the driver's seat, arms crossed, eyes closed, pretending to be asleep.

I had done all the hard work and Mel, who had monitored their progress across the fields from the car, had copped the arrests.

As Queen Victoria would have said, "We are not amused."

At the end of the day we had carried out our duty and probably prevented what could have been a serious rail accident.

A FOGGY NIGHT

It seemed in the 1950s and 1960s the fog, well could be better described as smog, was more frequent and a lot worse than today. On several occasions our patrol car was grounded and we only turned out in extreme emergencies.

On the night in question Mel and I were in the Control Room as it was a real 'peasouper' outside when the call came in, a motorist thought there was a sack of potatoes or something similar in the roadway on the Missenden bypass.

It was a long and tiring journey to get there as we almost felt our way along the A413. There, under a bridge, we found not a sack of potatoes but a young man. He had jumped off the bridge in an attempt to commit suicide but in doing so broke both his legs and fractured his pelvis.

We immediately called an ambulance and all we could do for him was try and keep him warm and speak words of encouragement, as he was still conscious. He must have been in terrible pain.

It seemed an eternity before the ambulance arrived and took him off to the hospital.

When I interviewed him a couple of days later he told me he had tried to kill himself as he had failed his exams and he was a disgrace and disappointment to his parents. What a terrible mental state he must have been in to take such drastic action.

I am pleased to say he made quite a reasonable recovery.

FATAL ACCIDENT AT STONE

When a person is killed in a road accident or in any other fatality it is a most distressing time for the next of kin. It can also be a distressing time for the other parties involved in, or who later deal with the accident.

As an example I will draw as a comparison the ripple effect of a stone being dropped into a pond. At the very centre are the closest relatives of the deceased, mother, father, wife, husband, etc. they suffer the most. The next ripple would be other close relatives, then further out those who were witnesses to the fatality, then those dealing with the aftermath, ambulance men, policemen, firemen, nurses and doctors, etc.

All those who have to deal with fatalities, no matter what their role, will to some degree be duly affected.

I attended an accident in Stone, about three miles west of Aylesbury. An 11 year old boy delivering newspapers rode his bike off the pavement into the path of a Land Rover.

I arrived at the scene shortly after the ambulance and by then the boy had been pronounced dead.

It fell to me to inform the parents of the tragedy and needless to say they were deeply shocked by the news.

Later that day I had to see the driver of the Land Rover. He was a farmer who had a farm situated halfway between the villages of Chearsley and Waddesdon.

When I got to the farmhouse I found the farmer was also in deep shock. He blamed himself for causing the boy's death, he said he should have anticipated the boy's movements, he should have been driving slower, and he should not have been going through the village so early in the morning. He was inconsolable; as he thought it was his fault the boy had died.

He was so distraught that on my advice his wife called out a doctor to give him a sedative. Due to his mental state I could not take a statement from him; he was practically incoherent with grief.

When I called on him a few days later he was no better, and he was still in a poor state when he had to attend the inquest a week or so later.

I kept in touch with the farmer for several months or so, (perhaps my farming instincts were coming out), he had lost all interest in his farm, would not drive on the roads or even drive his tractor in the fields.

A year on and he sold the farm and retired. There is no doubt that the accident had a profound effect on his mind.

MAKING A RUN FOR IT

As any police constable will vouch, police work does not come in a steady stream, hectic action is tempered with periods of inactivity. Often on nights the whole eight hour shift can be totally devoid of action, in fact it can be boring, so a bit of excitement occasionally is welcome during these period of quiet.

Just after 10pm Mel and I left the Traffic Headquarters at Walton Grove, Aylesbury, drove through the town and were leaving Aylesbury on the Oxford Road. A car in front, a Ford Escort that was doing a steady thirty miles per hour on this restricted road, suddenly speeded up and raced away up to about 60 mph. Something had spooked the driver and we wanted to know what; had he just committed a robbery, stolen the car or committed some other sin? We set off in pursuit.

The Escort then turned left towards Southcourt and from then on the driver, trying to lose us, drove like a madman. He drove over kerbs, onto and over the roundabouts, up streets the wrong way, crossed main roads at high speed. He was driving like a man possessed. On the other hand, I was not prepared to drive that low-slung Jaguar patrol car over kerbs, risking tearing off the exhaust pipe or bursting a tyre, so the other driver had an advantage over us from the outset.

As soon as the chase began Mel had called through to Headquarters asking for details of the registered owner of the car.

In the days before the Driver and Vehicle Licensing Centre, Swansea, and computerised records, local vehicle details were kept at the Aylesbury County Hall and the police had a key to the Licensing Department for use in an emergency, and at our request the duty sergeant had obtained details of the registered owner. He lived in Southcourt, Aylesbury.

In view of the dangerous situation we abandoned the chase and instead drove to the address of the registered owner, parked up a side road and with lights doused, waited and watched.

About half an hour later the car in question drove slowly along the street with its lights out and onto the drive of the owner's house and stopped. No doubt the driver did not want to alert the occupants that he had taken their car. The driver sat in the car for a several minutes, probably to let his blood pressure drop. We walked quietly to the back of the car and waited, then as he got out and very quietly closed the car door. Mel said,

"Nice evening for a drive sir."

He spun round and was confronted much to his shock and dismay by two police constables. He was duly arrested.

Now an interesting situation arose; the car belonged to his father. The lad was sixteen years of age, obviously had not passed his driving test therefore was not insured. In view of his tender age his parent had to be present during the interview at the police station.

Initially, Dad wanted to protect his son and we could see he was considering saying his son was driving the car with his permission but we pointed out that in such a case he, the father, would be charged with permitting his son to use the car without insurance.

He was in a cleft stick, either the father made a statement that he permitted the uninsured use of the car by his son or he made a statement that his son had stolen the car from him. After some thought the father took the right decision and decided on the second option.

In due course the lad appeared in court on numerous offences, convicted and disqualified for a year although he did not hold a licence.

A MAN OF INTERGRITY

I have lost count of the number of times a member of the public facing the possibility of prosecution would say he/she was a friend of the chief constable or he/she played golf with my superintendent, hoping I would let him/her off.

From the early 1950's to 1968 the chief constable of the Buckinghamshire Constabulary was Brigadier John Norman Cheney.

A former high ranking army officer, he was a man of vast experience and a real gentleman. I was not involved in the following incident but it was related to me by the constable who was.

In the mid 1950's Brigadier Cheney lived at Great Missenden, and on a Saturday, whilst off duty he left his house, drove his private car down a hill towards the A413, failed to stop at the main road and crashed into another car.

The police were called and my colleague Tony attended. At that time he was a young probationer and this was his first accident. Fancy your own chief constable being involved in your initiation accident!

Tony obtained the details of the driver whom the chief constable had crashed into and then he had to deal with the Chief, who he thought looked familiar.

On obtaining the driver's details Tony then knew he was dealing with his own chief constable, just to give him more reason to panic.

Brigadier Cheney realised how inexperienced the constable was so he set about 'advising' him what to do.

He asked the constable whom he considered would appear to be at fault and somewhat hesitantly, Tony said, "You are". Brigadier Cheney then told Tony to carry out his duty and report him for reckless, dangerous or careless driving and caution him, which the constable duly did.

When this matter came to court Brigadier Cheney sat in the dock, heard the evidence given against him (in those days statements were not read out in court, it was always personal attendance by all witnesses).

He pleaded guilty and then went on to praise Tony for the efficient way he had dealt with the accident.

A lot of influential people and of high standing and importance would try to wriggle out of a prosecution, not Brigadier Cheney.

A TELEVISION FOR THE CHIEF

Another little incident comes to mind about Brigadier Cheney. In addition to being chief constable of the Buckinghamshire Constabulary he was one of the Queen's ceremonial bodyguards and quite often had to go to important functions in which the Queen was involved where he wore some fancy uniform, buckled shoes, top coat and a funny hat.

On these days when he could not get to his office in Aylesbury, the office went to him. About 4pm, the duty patrol car crew would pick up the despatches from his office, together with the Times newspaper, and deliver them to his house near Great Missenden.

On carrying out this duty one sunny day, the chief constable asked me to walk with him round his substantial gardens. He appeared to be somewhat deep in thought, I assumed about his royal duties. Then unexpectedly he asked me,

"Do you have a television?"

I replied,

"Yes sir." (We had a second hand Bush nine inch black and white television at that time, gifted by my wife's parents).

We walked along for a short time then he asked,

"Do you think I should have one?"

This was a loaded question as in those days not many people had televisions and there was a strong field of thought that televisions were a waste of time, bad for your eyes, addled your brain, corrupted the viewers and generally was bad for your health and wellbeing.

After due consideration I told the chief constable that

there were some good news programmes on the television, it brought events, topical, historical and educational from the other side of the world into your front room, also there were some good programmes on gardening by a certain Percy Thrower. I knew the chief was a keen gardener. He walked on a bit further and then said,

"Thank you, I will take your advice and buy one."

It's nice to know I may have taken a part in widening my chief constable's horizons.

A WORRIED WIFE

It is not only the policemen who have all the worries; their wives are also subject to stress. In those days and before mobile phones and very few house phones they had no idea what their husbands were involved in whilst they were at work but they were aware that their hubbies were sometimes placed in dangerous situations.

It was whilst Mel and I were working the 2pm to 10pm shift that my wife Gerry had real cause for concern.

We were living at 83 Priory Crescent, about three miles from the police garage at Walton Grove, Aylesbury.

Gerry, for some reason, wanted to use the car that day so she took me to work at 2pm and she was to pick me up at Walton Grove at 10pm.

As it occasionally does, the emergency call came in requesting us to deal with an accident just as we were making our way back to Walton Grove to clock off. I had no way of letting Gerry know I would be late.

When Gerry got to Walton Grove at 10pm all the building lights were out so she parked in the car park, switched off the car lights and awaited my arrival. As time passed, 10:30pm, then 10:45pm she began to worry.

To compound her worries just before 11pm a breakdown truck carrying a very badly mangled Jaguar police car turned into the drive followed by another patrol car.

As the breakdown driver began to unload the wreckage Gerry did not know what to do. Had I been in the car at the time of the crash? Was I in hospital or worse?

Should she appear out of the dark and ask questions, did she really want to hear what could be very bad news about her husband?

She eventually plucked up enough courage to ask the police constable with the breakdown vehicle if I had been involved only to be told it was not me. I arrived shortly afterwards to reassure a very relieved Gerry.

The crashed Jaguar had been driven by a sergeant from Bletchley. At a crossroads he had left the road at a very fast speed and the car rolled over several times. Fortunately, the occupants were not seriously injured thanks to the sturdy build of the car and seat belts.

GOOD AND NOT SO GOOD

Most people we police constables meet are good people, thank goodness. I have been fortunate to be associated with too many good people to count and some have remained lifelong friends. Even today, some 58 years after I joined the police I have friends whom I met when I first enlisted. Then there are people you meet on the way, who through their sheer personality remain just as a very pleasant memory.

One such person was Pat Moss, the sister of the racing driver Stirling Moss. Pat remains as an example of one of my good memories although there is no reason why she should remember me.

In the early 1960's the Buckinghamshire Constabulary used the 2.4 Jaguar patrol cars. By today's standards they were not particularly fast, they could just about reach 100 mph, not fast enough to catch a Lotus Cortina or a Mini Cooper; indeed a lot of foreign cars would show the Jaguar a clean pair of heels.

I was following this funny little bulbous car along the Tring Road, Aylesbury, at the regulation 30 mph, when it reached the end of the limit, it streaked off into the distance; I accelerated the Jaguar as hard as I could but could not keep up with it. It slowed for the 30 mph limit at Aston Clinton and I then took the opportunity to pull in the driver – Pat Moss. She told me it was a works rally car made by SAAB and owned by a certain Mr Erik Carlsson. Pat Moss married Erik Carlsson in 1963.

That little car, the 96 model, had an 841cc three cylinder two- stroke engine coupled to a three speed gearbox. I was amazed that such a little car could generate so much acceleration and speed to leave behind a 2.4 litre Jaguar.

Pat Moss in her most charming way showed us over the car and invited us to try it out. I was very impressed, both by the car and its driver.

A few years later I purchased a rally SAAB 96 and then bought one for my wife. I have owned in total four of these little two stroke cars and loved them all.

What a pity two stroke cars are not made today.

A couple of years after I first met Pat Moss the Constabulary upgraded the Traffic Department to the 3.4 model Jaguars, a vastly superior vehicle capable of reaching 110mph, a whole 10 mph faster.

THE FANCIFUL CONSTABLE

During our break on early shifts breakfast was usually taken at the canteen in Exchange Street Police Station in Aylesbury. This gave us a chance to talk to other officers and swap information.

One day Mel and I went into the canteen and one of the beat constables, Jeremy Byron was there.

Now Jeremy, allegedly a very intelligent man, was a bit odd to say the least. On one occasion we asked him what he had done at the weekend and he said that he had a call from the White House in Washington seeking his services.

He agreed and they sent a fighter plane all the way from the USA to Haddenham Airfield to pick up Jeremy, fly him to America where he acted as interpreter in a spy case and then fly him home again on the Sunday so that he was ready for duty on the Monday.

He said that due to the high secrecy of the case the CIA did not use their interpreters but preferred to fly Jeremy all the way to America to carry out this task.

Jeremy always had these high-powered weekends and he must have travelled all over the world at the behest of various governments.

He talked in such a convincing way it was difficult to tell fact from fiction. I personally just did not believe his stories and thought he was a dreamer.

On one occasion after listening to one of Jeremy's exploits, I had just finished breakfast when the reserve officer called up to say that an Italian lady who did not speak a word of English was at the front desk and he needed help.

I went down with Jeremy to the front office and to my surprise he started to interpret apparently with no trouble at all. So he was not as fanciful as everyone thought.

Apparently, Jeremy spoke several languages fluently and he was a good interpreter. As time went by we who knew him realised he had hidden depths but I still believe he was a good storyteller and the stories he related whilst we partook of our breakfasts were a lot of baloney. Jeremy died in late 2008.

ACCIDENT AT STEWKLEY

An accident that occurred during the late evening on a bend outside the village of Stewkley would appear, on the face of it, to be straightforward and routine. A lady driving the family car failed to make a left hand bend and crashed into a tree. When the police and ambulance arrived she was pronounced dead.

We estimated from the damage to the car the impact speed would have been between 20 and 25mph. There were no skid marks.

However, there were some discrepancies, the injuries to her head were to the back rather than the front and there was a smear of blood on the fascia in front of the passenger seat.

The post mortem revealed some other enlightening facts. Although she was not wearing a seat belt and the impact would have thrown her forward and her chest would have been the first part of her body to hit (with some force) the steering wheel, there were no marks on her chest.

At this stage of the enquiry the C.I.D were informed and a detective inspector took over the enquiry.

A blood test showed that the smear of blood on the

passenger side was her blood, so how did it get there?

When we saw her husband to tell him of the tragic death of his wife he showed the usual signs of distress.

The husband said that his wife had left to make a visit to her sister who lived in Stewkley. This did not ring true, why would she leave the house so late in the evening to make an unscheduled visit to her sister?

Enquiries with the sister revealed that no arrangement had been made for them to meet and the sister also told us that the deceased and her husband had a stormy and sometimes violent marriage.

When we spoke to a neighbour we learnt that on the night of the accident there were sounds of an almighty row at the deceased's house and a car was later heard driving away.

The detective inspector and I re-interviewed the husband but he denied being involved in his wife's death. When asked to open his shirt we saw a welt mark across his chest exactly where a seat belt would have been (air bags were not fitted in those days.)

He then admitted that after a violent row he had hit his wife in anger over the head with an object and inadvertently killed her.

He had carried her body out of the house and placed

her in the passenger seat and then, after tightly fitting his own seat belt he had deliberately driven into the tree, got out and moved his wife into the driver's seat and left the scene.

Just to tidy things up we took possession of his shoes and matched them with shoe prints found in the soft soil near the scene of the accident. He was duly convicted of the killing of his wife.

Surprisingly this murder, classified later as manslaughter, received very little publicity prior to or during the short trial at which the husband pleaded guilty.

ACC AND PANDA CARS

The introduction in 1965 of the Panda Car into the policing methods had a very profound effect not only in the way the police worked but also on the general public.

The Lancashire Police was the first force to put the panda, sometimes referred to as a jam sandwich, onto the roads and other forces quickly followed this move.

Its introduction was heralded as a good move forward but I had my doubts then, and still do. I believe it was a step backwards.

The theory was that three country beats could cover a large rural area and would be amalgamated, the three police offices would be closed forever, two of the constables would revert to working town beats and the remaining constable would work the three beats from a panda car.

One advantage of the panda car system however was that they were equipped with radios connected to the headquarters control room. Up to the time of the introduction of the panda car, as a general rule only the traffic patrol cars were fitted with radios.

I, with about fifty other police officers attended a meeting with the assistant chief constable of the Buckinghamshire Constabulary who was a former assistant commissioner of the Metropolitan Police.

This ACC claimed the panda system was his brainchild and it would work. In effect he dared any of the officers present at that meeting to challenge his new plan. He said that the panda car would be like a mobile police office.

Not surprisingly, there were lots of objections to his panda car scheme and these he batted aside as if they were of no consequence.

He said that a panda car would reach the scene of an incident faster than a constable walking or cycling, the high profile of the panda car would be reassuring to the public and he put forward many other factors that supported his scheme.

One fact he had not taken into account or ignored was that previously for most days there was twenty four hour cover by the three beat officers doing eight hours each, with his scheme there would only be eight hours cover with the one beat officer in a panda car in the twenty four hour period covering three beats, but he would not be detracted from pushing forward his plans.

A suggestion that members of the public are more inclined to talk to a patrolling constable than they would to a constable driving past in a panda car at 30mph was another argument that he totally rejected.

In answer to other questions he said that he would not expect the panda car to leave its beat except on every fourth or fifth day to return to the nearest town to refuel, pick up despatches, or, if the officer had carried out an arrest to take the prisoner to the nearest station.

When one constable asked him what he should do when he had to deal with a large and violent dog? Was he expected to carry a rabid dog around with him until the next time he had cause to go to the nearest main police station? The assistant chief constable did not have an answer to that question.

The presence of the panda car, now in various guises, can be seen both in the country, towns and cities; meanwhile the bobby on the beat is a rarity. What a shame.

AN INCAUTIOUS WORD

An incautious word or two can cause embarrassment as my mate Mel found out one night.

Mel and I were on patrol and had reached the end of our beat at the Buckinghamshire and Bedfordshire borders at the Travellers Rest, near Eddlesborough. Instead of retracing our steps towards Aylesbury we decided to cut through a bit of Bedfordshire so we drove through Eddlesborough, Slapton and into Leighton Buzzard.

About 4am at the bottom of Leighton Buzzard High Street we met up with the Bedfordshire Traffic car. After a bit of chatter and comparing our respective patrol cars, one of the Bedfordshire coppers said,

"I understand you have a new assistant chief

constable, how's he fitting in?"

Mel replied, "Not at all, he's a right flipping waste of time," (or in words vaguely similar.)

This comment stunned the Bedfordshire coppers for a few moments, then, one of them said,

"He's my dad."

Now Mel on the way back to Aylesbury was unusually quiet which was hardly surprising.

A BIT OF RALLYING

Life was not all work and no fun and most policemen had hobbies, mine was motor sport, using a Mini 850 that I bought in early 1960, then later, a SAAB 96.

In 1958, together with some other officers we formed the Buckinghamshire Constabulary Motor Club and we competed in rallies, hill climbs and auto tests with which I can claim some success.

A year later all the countries police motor clubs got together and formed the Federation of British Police Motor Clubs and this widened our horizons somewhat. So much so that in 1962 I was chosen to represent the Federation in an International Police Rally in Belgium and we were supplied with a works rally prepared Riley 1.5 and Sergeant Cyril Wise was to be my navigator.

After a week's reconnaissance in Belgium, little bits of Holland and France, we were ready for the big event. This was exciting stuff.

Over one hundred cars competed in this rally representing practically every country in Europe. As well as us from England with four work's cars, there were work's teams from Sweden, Italy, France and Germany.

On the Saturday the rally started and the next twenty four hours were a blur as we travelled over 800 miles with just two half hour breaks for sustenance and refuelling.

One memory was an incident on the Chimay Race Circuit just over the border in France. This was a Special Stage where we had to complete one lap against the clock, timed to the second and the cars started one minute apart.

On the start line in front of us was Jaguar. We could hardly see it as a thick blanket of fog had descended on the racetrack.

It was then our turn, on the drop of the flag we were off, the fog was so thick Cyril was looking out of the passenger window calling if I got too near to the left of the track whilst I was looking out of the right driver's door window, it was no good looking through the windscreen.

After a few hair raising moments we managed to complete the lap with a reasonably good time. A few minutes later the Jaguar that had started a minute before us came in, we must have overtaken it somewhere, or more likely the driver had meandered off the circuit.

At the end of the rally and on the Sunday there was a banquet and prize giving. During the prize giving I had no idea what was going on as all the announcements were in French, then I heard the names Wode and Wheeze called (Wood and Wise). Cyril and I realised that we must have won something so we went onto the podium and were presented with horrible looking blue vases. We later learnt that with two other Riley drivers we had won the manufacturer's team prize.

My wife Gerry shared my view that it was a very unattractive vase and after a couple of years it vanished, I do not know where, but I suspect my wife may know!

But more important to me and an object I cherished was a very nice little medallion with the Riley emblem on it presented to the winning team by the Riley Car

Company in appreciation of our efforts.

The Riley Car Company no longer exists and another manufacturers name that has sunk into history.

OOPS – WATCH THAT DROP

Two years later I was again competing in this rally with a works MGB, a lovely car and we were doing quite well and in with a chance of winning our class until we were nearing Dinant.

We were on a 'timed to a second' special stage going down a steep winding hill with a high bank on the left and a big drop to the right.

Cyril was a first class navigator and kept me on course and with his stopwatch, calculator and other devices also kept me up to time until I realised a corner I was approaching was sharper than the others and I was going too fast. I slammed on the brakes; we skidded across the road and stopped with the back wheels on the verge and the front of the car out in space, balanced in the top of a fir tree.

The car was teetering on the brink of a huge drop of at least thirty feet; it was a really scary moment. We were in trouble.

Much to our surprise despite being in a fairly remote location and it was nearing midnight; half a dozen men appeared from goodness knows where and manhandled the car back onto the road. With hurried thanks we were on our way.

We reached the end of the special section at Dinant but due to my mistake incurred a six minute penalty and that was the end of our chances of finishing on the podium.

That was the sort of excitement I did not want to experience again.

HOLY COW!

Early one morning Mel and I got a call to attend an accident on the A41 Ludgershall Straight between Waddesdon and Bicester. A car had run into a cow that had strayed onto the highway. Cows are pretty solid and it is amazing how much damage they can do to a car.

After dealing with the accident and getting the manager of Waddesdon Estate to arrange removal of the dead cow I had to consider further court action against the owner of the cow for allowing it to stray on the highway.

My enquiries suggested the owner was Lady Rothschild from Waddesdon Manor, the Chairman of Aylesbury Magistrates Court.

Later that day I telephoned the Estate Manager to ask for arrangement to be made so that I could interview Lady Rothschild and report her for process so that a summons could be issued.

When I arrived at the appointed time she was not there. The Estate Manager told me that she was not the owner of the dead cow as it, and a couple of other cows, had been sold by Lady Rothschild to him, the Estate Manager a few months previously. This was very convenient I must say. He showed me a receipt to support this claim.

The Estate Manager took full responsibility for the cow and the accident and he was duly convicted. I knew it was a set up, I also firmly believe that Lady Rothschild did not even know about the accident, and the following deception was carried out without her knowledge.

Her integrity was such that she would not allow anyone to pervert the course of justice. As the case was heard at Brill Magistrate's Court and not at her court she probably did not hear about the outcome.

NAUGHTY LADS

Most police officers I have met over my thirty years in the police force are good and conscientious but there are always a few who will swing the lead. There was one such couple on Aylesbury Traffic but obviously no names will be mentioned.

One member of this crew was courting a girl from the typing pool at the Police Headquarters and then his crewmate formed an alliance with another girl from the same typing pool.

When on nights, at least once a week these two officers would patrol until about midnight, by which time the streets were quiet, then they would go to where the two girls shared a flat and the officers would spend the night with them.

They had an arrangement whereby the officer on the switchboard at Aylesbury control room would in an emergency give one ring on the telephone to the girl's flat alerting the officers to return to the patrol car, take a radio call and deal with whatever required their attention.

The other constables on Aylesbury Traffic knew what was going on but I do not believe it reached the ears of the sergeants.

This couple had the luck of the devil. My crewmate Mel and I went about our duties with due diligence but most nights were, as far as arrests were concerned, quite fruitless but this philandering couple would on the way back to the station after a night of fun often run across a stolen car or a burglar.

THE FLAGSTAFF MOTEL

The above story reminds me of a little incident of a similar nature that occurred in America.

My wife Gerry and I were touring with our friends Vivian and Gene and stopped overnight at a motel in Flagstaff, Arizona. After retiring for the night I did not sleep very well so about 5:30.am I got up to go for a walk.

As I walked out of the motel I was surprised to see at least eight police cars, both State and Highway Patrol were parked outside. I wondered what major incident was happening inside the motel to warrant so much police attention.

At breakfast that morning I mentioned this to Gene and he allayed my fears that there had not been a murder or some other dark deed taking place close to where we had been sleeping.

It appears to be the norm, not only in Flagstaff but also in many parts of the United States, for officers on night duty to retire to motels with free accommodation when the rest of the population had gone to bed. The officers were contactable either by phone or radio so this practice appeared to be acceptable to the senior officers.

I must add that I was not aware whether or not our colleagues on the American side of the Atlantic were ensconced with females.

No way could I envisage this happening in good old Blighty.

THE GREAT TRAIN ROBBERY

It was at 6am on the morning of 8th August 1963 that I was awoken from my slumbers by someone knocking loudly on the door of my house, it was my traffic sergeant. He told me that a train had been robbed on my beat and over a million pounds stolen. The Great Train Robbery had just taken place. I was urgently required to report for duty.

For the next few months Mel and I were glorified chauffeurs in our Jaguar patrol cars for the senior CID officers of the Buckinghamshire Constabulary and the Metropolitan Police investigating this crime.

The police operation was highly successful and it is believed that only two of the original gang escaped prosecution by escaping overseas.

Of the £2,631.684 stolen (equivalent to £41,000,000 today) about three quarters of a million pounds was recovered.

One of the traffic officer's tasks was to pick up the prisoners, as and when they were arrested and convey them to Aylesbury Police Station including transporting exhibits and carry out any other such duties. It was quite a hectic few months.

During this time we got to know all of the robbers quite well. Some members of the public and the press may have expressed a grudging admiration of the robbers for their audacity in executing the robbery, we knew them as a bunch of vicious and unscrupulous thugs who deserved the heavy penalties imposed on them.

Of the fifteen arrested, eleven were convicted of a number of criminal offences and sent to prison for between 3 and 30 years.

On 7th August 2013, a Commemorative Anniversary Dinner was held at Eynsham Hall, near Witney, Oxfordshire, hosted by Sarah Thornton, the chief constable of the Thames Valley Police, to which my wife and I were invited.

There, I was presented with a Chief Constable's Commendation for my dedication to duty and service on the Great Train Robbery enquiry. I was one of only seventeen so awarded, still alive, from the original enquiry team.

This event was covered by both local and national television.

THE GREAT TRAIN ROBBERS

So what happened to The Great Train Robbers after release from prison? This is a question I am occasionally asked; well here's the story so far.

1. Bruce Reynolds, escaped from prison, went to Mexico, Canada and France. He was re-arrested in 1968. After his release he was again arrested in 1980 for dealing in drugs. He died in February 2011, aged 81 years.

2. Dennis Goody now lives overseas.

3. Charles Wilson was shot and died in Spain.

4. Ronald Edwards committed suicide in 1994.

5. Brian Field died in a car crash in 1997.

6. Ronald Biggs, after being on the run for many years, gave himself up when he returned to England. He was finally released from prison in 2009. He died in 2013.

7. Roy James was sentenced for a second time, for attempted murder. He has also died.

8. Robert Welch was released from prison in 1976.

9. Roger Cordery, released from prison rejoined the family florist business.

10. Thomas Wisby, was jailed again in 1989 for dealing in drugs.

TRAFFIC – BLETCHLEY

In December 1966 I was posted to Bletchley Traffic Department. This traffic department consisted of two sergeants and eight constables and we had three patrol cars, two Jaguar 3.4's and a Ford Granada Estate that was used mainly for motorway patrol. The estate car was handy for carrying the vast amount of equipment that may be required at the scene of a motorway accident.

I had to quickly learn my way round north Buckinghamshire but more importantly I had to know how to deal with emergencies on the M1 Motorway. Those high speed accidents and other incidents required an entirely new policing technique as wrong or slow action could end in a very nasty situation. In fact just before I joined Bletchley Traffic a traffic sergeant was killed whilst dealing with an accident on the M1.

Initially, I was teamed up with Geordie whom I did not get on with. He was a scrounger and lazy and would whenever possible get out of dealing with any incident on the motorway.

After a couple of months I managed to get away from him and was then teamed up with Ernie.

Ernie was an ex RAF man who was a serving officer in the Air Training Corps, he sported a handlebar moustache and really looked the part.

We got on well despite the fact he was not keen on confrontations of a nasty nature – he liked the quiet life. We were crewmates from March 1967 until my promotion in March 1969.

A BIT TOO FAST

The excitement of the chase can overcome caution as was brought home to me very forcibly when I realised how near my colleague and I could have been to having a major accident.

We had a problem with motorists on the M1 motorway travelling at excessive speed and I mean excessive. We were determined to do something about it. Our 3.4 Jaguar patrol cars were capable of no more than 110 mph, not fast enough to keep up with some of the modern sports cars.

In 1967 the Traffic Department at Bletchley loaned from the Jaguar Car Company an 'E' type Jaguar for patrol purposes. This Jaguar was a plain red car and other than blue lights the police garage installed in the front windscreen and a siren it looked like any other private sports car. The only other non-standard feature was a calibrated speedometer.

I was driving this Jaguar with Ernie as my observer along the middle lane of the M1 motorway at the legal speed of 70 mph when another 'E' type came past us at well over 100 mph. I set off in pursuit and I had just started to match its speed for the purpose of checking it over a three mile distance (that took about one and a half minutes), when the driver, obviously seeing another 'E' type behind him and being of a competitive nature, started to accelerate so off we went after him. Eventually, we recorded his speed at 130 mph over five miles. This is the fastest I had ever driven.

Shortly after this chase Ernie and I had a call from the control room that there was a piece of timber on the carriageway of the M1. We went to the location given and saw a thick bulk of timber, probably part of a railway sleeper in the outside (fast) lane which cars were swerving round.

We had to run across three lanes of fast moving traffic and this meant good judgement and the ability to run – very fast.

We moved the bulk of timber from the carriageway onto the central reservation. I then realised this piece of wood was on the same stretch of motorway that half an hour earlier the speeding motorist and I had driven along at 130 mph.

What would have happened if that lump of timber had just been dropped from a lorry onto the fast lane thirty minutes earlier just as the speeding motorist, my partner and I had been travelling along at such a fast speed? It does not bear thinking about.

He was stopped, reported and sent for prosecution.

When he appeared at Newport Pagnell Magistrate's Court he pleaded not guilty. I recall this wealthy and rather arrogant young man saying to the Magistrates in his defence, in what I can only say in a disdainful way, something like,

"Minions like you who will never drive an expensive car like an 'E' type, would not know that the difference between 70 mph and 130 mph is no more than the twinkle of the toe."

That did not go down well and I am sure the Magistrates upped the fine as he was heavily fined and disqualified.

A SWEEPING SITUATION

Mentioning danger on the motorway reminds me of another incident on the M1. This was before the central barriers were installed and the only thing to stop cars from crossing the central reservation was a not very effective bed of shingle.

A car had crossed over the central reservation and in doing so spread a huge swathe of shingle over two of the carriageways and this had caused quite a few cars to have their windscreens shattered.

Ernie and I arrived, coned off the fast and middle lane and with brooms (part of the motorway car's equipment) started to sweep the fast lane clear of the shingle.

After a couple of minutes I thought this is not right I am working with my back to approaching traffic. I then, with broom over my shoulder, walked about 150 yards to the other end of the coned off area and had just started to sweep up the shingle when a car burst through the cones at the other end, the driver lost control on the loose shingle and headed straight towards me. Rapid avoiding action was taken.

If I had not, a few minutes earlier, realised the danger

I was in by having my back to the approaching traffic and moving to the other end there is no doubt I would have been hit by the car that must have been doing close to 70 mph. Phew! Another narrow escape.

DRIVING FOR PLEASURE

When I was called to the scene of an accident at Newport Pagnell I expected it to be a road traffic accident, this particular one was not. It was a garage accident.

A gentleman in his early eighties and his seventy five year old girl friend had been to the local pond to feed the ducks, then on returning home he had driven onto the driveway and stopped facing his open garage. He asked his girlfriend to get out and put the kettle on for a cup of tea whilst he garaged the car.

His girlfriend was halfway out of the car when it shot forward, into the garage, dragging her with it. The car hit the back of the garage with a might whack, partly demolishing the wall. Unfortunately, the girl friend, dragged into the garage by the car received serious injuries. The lady was taken to hospital.

The driver was in such a state of shock that he was not in a condition to be interviewed at that time. This suited me; as I was due to take a two weeks holiday.

On return from holiday I saw the couple at their flat just as a matter of routine as strictly speaking, as it occurred on private property, it was not a reportable traffic accident.

I asked the man to produce his driving licence, he showed me his bus pass and then, when asked to produce his certificate of insurance he showed me a letter from Meals on Wheels. He was not 'with it'.

At this point the girl friend found his driving licence and asked me then and there to cut it up and send it to the DVLA as she said he was not going to drive again.

The man made a short statement authorising me to cut up his licence and send it to Swansea. His girlfriend was right his driving days were over.

Next I went to the garage where the car had been taken, to find out the extent of the damage to the car. At this point I was being helpful to the couple and I wanted to see if the car could be repaired or salvaged in any way so they could recoup something from this tragic accident. It was a total mess.

Whilst talking to the mechanic he told me that although the car, a little FIAT automatic had only covered 2,000 miles he had already fitted three new sets of brake pads.

The mechanic told me that he tried to explain to the old gentleman when he bought the car how an automatic gearbox worked, as there were only two pedals and how he should drive it.

The poor man could not comprehend the instruction so he devised his own method of driving. He would put it into gear, accelerate away and keeping the throttle in the same position no matter what his speed or the driving conditions were, and then as much as possible regulate the car's speed by using just the brakes instead of the throttle. No wonder the brakes wore out so quickly. Unbelievable.

It was a good job that the gentleman only drove it three times a week to the local pond so they could feed the ducks. I suppose that is a good enough reason to have a car.

I hope someone else took on the task of feeding the ducks.

THE TERRITORIAL ARMY

After my move to Bletchley in 1966 I decided to join the Territorial Army. This was allowed under the Police Regulations on the understanding that the police service overrode any army commitments.

I should add that I had previous army experience as I had served with the Bedfordshire and Hertfordshire Regiment during the Suez crisis in Egypt from 1951 to 1953.

I joined the Oxfordshire and Buckinghamshire Light Infantry at Bletchley as an Under Officer. The first thing that came to my attention was that the whole unit was a shambles. There was no structured training and the paperwork was in a mess so over the first few months I set about sorting out and devising a filing system and then worked out a training programme.

The Unit Commander was a Captain and unknown to me was shortly to retire. He did not tell me at the time that he had put my name forward to the Army Headquarters suggesting I was promoted and took over the unit at Bletchley.

After an interview at the Army Headquarters at Aylesbury I went on an Officer Training Course at

Frimley, Surrey, passed and was promoted to Second Lieutenant (later Lieutenant) and I then took charge of the Bletchley Unit.

In connection with my TA duties I was expected to attend an evening parade on average once a week, no problem there but for the two weeks annual camp I had to take my annual leave from the police so there was no holiday for my wife, but in those days when money was short it was good to get two salaries, one police and one army for a couple of weeks.

Whilst at the annual camp in Shropshire one of my lads on an evening off got into a fight with some locals in the nearby town of Oswestry. He took a swing at a local lad who ducked and my lad gave a brick wall a mighty clout. He was taken to the Shrewsbury hospital for treatment to his badly injured hand whilst I, as Duty Officer, was called out to sort out the fracas with the local police.

Later I went to the hospital where the injured lad was being treated. The nurse said he would have to have a tetanus jab. I told him, "drop your trousers," something he was very reluctant to do, he was not so brave now but the nurse much to my chagrin decided to inject into his arm.

A few days later I was helping to load a large wooden canoe onto an army lorry; my fingers got trapped and were badly cut. It was my turn to go to the same hospital for treatment.

After being bandaged that same nurse said I had to have a tetanus jab; I was about to roll up my sleeve when she said, "drop your trousers." She had a twinkle in her eye as she inserted the needle into my backside.

The incident in Oswestry was resolved satisfactorily thanks to my police knowledge and army experience. I suggested to the Shropshire Police that if they did not want to charge my men who were involved in the fight but let the army meet out their own justice that would be instant and more severe. They agreed.

This suggestion saved that county a lot of money and when the troublemakers came up before the Commanding Officer, they were confined to barracks for the rest of the fortnight and given other punishments as well. A good result all round.

AMALGAMATION

On 1st April 1968 my beloved force, the Buckinghamshire Constabulary ceased to exist when it was amalgamated along with the Oxfordshire Constabulary, Berkshire Constabulary, Reading

Borough Police and the City of Oxford Police, into the Thames Valley Police.

I realised that my dream of spending the last fifteen years as a village bobby in rural Buckinghamshire had diminished somewhat as that melting pot of police forces could throw up all sorts of problems; my future was now in doubt. I also realised that from the date of amalgamation the term police constable was not used so often in police circles, as I was now a police officer.

ASSIMILATION

Shortly after amalgamation I received joining instructions for an assimilation course at the new Force Training Centre at Sulhamstead, some five miles from Reading.

Accompanying the joining instructions was a map of the area showing the nearest village, Theale. I was discussing travel arrangements with another rustic copper at Bletchley when, looking at the map he said,

"Oh, I see the map shows the nearest pub, The Ale, that's considerate of them." Looking at my map I retorted that no pub was shown on my mine. He then said,

"Look, there, it says The Ale."

I am still unsure if he was pulling my leg or did he really believed that Theale was a public house!

HORSES FOR COURSES

After the joining of the five forces, the Thames Valley Police announced that a Mounted Branch would be formed based at the new city of Milton Keynes.

My sergeant suggested that I, as the son of a farmer and a rustic type of copper, would be ideal for the job and should put my name forward as a candidate for this new Branch. Perhaps the sergeant wanted to get rid of me!

I gave due consideration to his suggestion but soon discounted it, as my short experience with horses on our farm were not happy ones, those beasts were dangerous at both ends and damned uncomfortable in the middle.

I preferred the horsepower supplied by the Jaguar patrol cars.

A CHIEF CONSTABLE AND A CHIEF CONSTABLE

Brigadier Cheney had been the chief constable of the Buckinghamshire Constabulary for about ten years and he was a fine chief, very popular and he looked after his men. He made a point of knowing both his constables and their wives and families. There were social events and sports days where he took the opportunity to meet his men. In the Buckinghamshire Constabulary it felt like we were one big family.

Brigadier Cheney retired in April 1968 when the Buckinghamshire Constabulary was merged into the Thames Valley Police. From then on there were a number of chief constables in the new force, it seemed they changed every two years or so as those high fliers used the force as a stepping stone to bigger forces that would give them larger salaries.

It was while I was in charge of the Motor Vehicle Investigation Squad that I received a call from the chief constable's aide to attend a press conference about vehicle theft at the Police Headquarters, Kidlington.

In preparation I armed myself with a large amount of data, charts facts and figures about current vehicle theft and associated topics just in case the press asked any difficult questions.

When I got to the conference room I saw there was quite a crowd; television, radio, local and national newspapers were well represented. On the top table were the chief constable's aide, the force press officer and I.

At exactly 10am the chief constable came in. Now at this point I must point out that I had not met this chief constable before as he had taken over the job about three months previously. I saw his aide point to me and say something, presumably saying who I was. He did not acknowledge my presence in any way.

The chief constable then read some notes from a printed script, said that he would not take any questions and just walked out. What sort of press conference was that?

I was not impressed by the way he treated the press or even me.

That feeling of really belonging was not there then or in fact during the rest of my service.

On the question of belonging and feeling part of a team, about three months prior to my retirement from the Thames Valley Police I sent a report to Headquarters of my intentions. The only response was a memo from the Finance Department informing me of my pension entitlement.

On 19th September 1986, after thirty years of service, I was in my office at Cumnor at 9am, spending most of the day tidying up the outstanding files and making notes for my successor. At 5pm, having emptied out the drawers of my desk, I shook hands with my colleagues and left for home.

It would have been nice to receive some recognition for my thirty years of service from any senior officers from the Thames Valley Police. It was as if I had not existed. No one called to see me or in any other way seemed interested.

THE AMERICAN WAY

In sharp contrast to the previous story, about two years later my friend Gene who was a detective constable in the California Highway Patrol in Visalia, retired and I went to his farewell party.

Gene had been a Marshall in California, then transferred to the California Highway Patrol and due to his experience with farm equipment was one of the foremost investigators into the theft of farm and contractors equipment in California.

On retirement his leaving party was held at the Holiday Inn in Visalia and was attended by the Chief of the California Highway Patrol, the Chief of Visalia City Police, local Sheriff, the Mayor and countless other important people.

He and his wife Vivian had been great friends to my wife and I, and we had holidayed with them in the United States, Europe and South Africa on at least a dozen occasions.

I flew to America for this event, it was a grand affair, people arrived by helicopter, light plane and other means and there must have been about one hundred people attending.

The California Highway Patrol paid for the whole event and he received numerous awards in appreciation of his service.

There was no doubt that Gene was a valued member of the CHP and every effort was made to make him feel that he belonged, so different to my retirement.

THE CITY OF OXFORD

In March 1969 I was promoted sergeant and posted to the City of Oxford where I took over 'A' Relief. I inherited fifteen constables, from the very experienced to the raw recruits just out of the training school so I had a mixed bag to get to know.

I was fortunate in having a first class inspector in Doug. He appreciated I was new to the task of being a sergeant and gave me every encouragement and advice.

The promotion and move to Oxford put the final spoke in the wheel of my desire to be a village bobby.

This was another time of intense learning as I had to get to know my men, the different patrol patterns, the beats, the locations of the thirty plus colleges and in fact I had to learn my way round the city.

Although amalgamation had taken place almost a year earlier, the City of Oxford methods were still to a certain extent vastly different in the way the police system worked compared to the rest of the Thames Valley Police, no doubt it was influenced by the fact it was a university city

THE TIMID BOXER

I had a good squad of police officers, most of them hard working and diligent but it must be expected there would always be one or two that were not up to scratch.

John Robson was a probationer that I had inherited when I took over A Relief. I soon realised that he was not turning in any process reports or making any arrests.

He was one of the few officers that always seemed to have trouble with his radio. I soon formed the opinion that he was a shirker who did not like confrontation. This was surprising as he was an amateur boxer and fought to good effect in the Police Championships in London.

On one occasion, I went to London with the Force Boxing Team to these championships, I saw him put up a good fight and he showed a lot of courage so why was he as ineffective as a constable?

As a sergeant it was my responsibility to submit appraisals on all my probationers and of course I had to report that I had warned John on two occasions that if his performance did not improve he would not be confirmed in his appointment.

John was a married man with two young sons and lived in a police house so I would have thought that to ensure his family's security it was in his own interest to succeed as a constable.

One afternoon I went to meet him on his beat in Oxford High Street. Initially, I could not find him and of course he did not answer his radio. Eventually, I found him in the deep recessed doorway of an empty shop so that he would not be visible to the public.

I gave him a good pep talk and then asked him what he would do if a member of the public reported a disturbance in a nearby street. He said he would go the other way; he said that if people started a disturbance then they should resolve it themselves. This was not the response I expected so he received a further and final warning.

In my final report on this probationer, after deep thought I reported the full and true facts; there is no room for police officers in the police who are not up to the job, and as a result he was dismissed from the force and told to vacate the police house.

On one hand I felt bad about this as I personally knew his wife and children and was aware my report would render them homeless, but on the other hand, he had received plenty of warnings that he was not up to the standard required of a police officer.

UNIVERSITY TYPES

About the same time I was promoted sergeant the Home Office introduced the fast promotion scheme for those with a university education. They were guaranteed promotion to sergeant after three years of service and to inspector after five, and from then on the sky was the limit.

I had two of these alleged high flyers on my relief. One of them was quite good, keen and energetic he would obviously make a good officer. The other, well, what could I say, I shall call him Laurie. Whilst he was with my relief he was mediocre to poor but despite my adverse reports he was destined under the scheme to be promoted.

After eleven months at Oxford I was appointed detective sergeant and took over the Car Squad so this meant I did not see Laurie through the final months of his probationary period.

Several years later I was in charge of a wide ranging operation involving heavy goods vehicles (see later about this operation). This was an operation that involved two other forces so the 'Powers That Be' decided a more senior officer should oversee the operation. This high-flying but unsatisfactory probationer, Laurie, now a superintendent was appointed as Officer in Charge.

About once a week he would visit the incident room at Faringdon police station, ask a few routine questions and have a cup of tea with a biscuit and go. At no time did he take charge of the operation, give advice or input into the investigation.

When the great day came and warrants were executed and the raids took place involving over 75 officers from three forces, he was no-where to be seen.

Perhaps I should not be too critical of this man as he could have been very good at administration or other desk jobs but certainly he was no good at the sharp end.

THE MEDIATOR

I do not know how but at Oxford I gained a reputation for being a mediator or perhaps nobody else wanted the job.

It was expected that a certain amount of friction would be caused between the police and the university heads due to the fact that some of those highly educated Dons, Proctors and Chancellors believed they were above the law in respect of how they drove and parked their cars.

When such persons were reported for motoring offences letters were soon on their way to the chief constable, they were redirected to the chief superintendent at Oxford City who in turn passed them on to me, a sergeant, for action.

The course of action I took depended on the seriousness of the offences or sometimes on the attitude of the complainant. If the offences were of a very minor nature and the complainant was prepared to accept a caution then that is what would happen.

However, if the motoring offences were more serious then in my diplomatic way I would point out the error of their ways and that they must accept that court proceedings would be taken against them.

Fortunately, during the twelve months I was at Oxford I only dealt with about eight of these more serious complaints, all I believe, successfully.

SPECIAL CONSTABLES

Inspector Doug was in charge of the Special Constables at Oxford and quite frankly the whole shebang was totally inadequate; it was how Doug had inherited it. He asked me to sort them out.

I reviewed the performance of the eighty or so special constables and found out that only about ten had donned their uniform and attended their allotted police station within the previous year. They were a lot of wasters; it was time for a cull.

Within a three month period I visited the malingerers and 'advised' them that unless they intended to attend the monthly training sessions I proposed to set up and were prepared to report for duty at least once a month they were out.

In any case several of them were too aged to serve as special constables; they held the post in name only.

Whether it would please the powers that be or not I relieved about sixty of them of their warrants and uniforms; in effect I had sacked them.

I have no idea what the chief superintendent at Oxford thought but I do know the chief superintendent of the Special Constabulary was not happy.

I then set up a monthly training programme at St Aldates Police Station using in-house instructors from the Training Department, Forensic Department, Fraud Squad, Firearms Squad, Dog Section, and Car Squad and from other departments.

This programme alone renewed the special constable's interest in police work and they once again became a valuable support to the regular police service.

ASCOT RACES

Whilst at Oxford I was allocated duty at Ascot Races, which is not a bad thing as it was a long day out with plenty of overtime, therefore more pay.

We left Oxford by coach about 4:30am and it would

be about 8pm before we left Ascot to travel back to Oxford. We had to be at Ascot about four hours before the first race to check security.

My team was allocated to the Silver Ring where a large number of the well to do congregate so I was able to mix with some quite famous people.

Before the first race, I briefly spoke to a bookie that was setting up his pitch. He showed me a telex he had just removed from an envelope. It showed just one word, the name of a horse. He said it was a good bet.

Later that morning I was speaking to one of the stewards and I told him that I was thinking of putting a bit of money on a horse and when I mentioned the one the bookie had recommended, he agreed it was a dead cert.

As a Police Officer in uniform and on duty I was not allowed to bet on the horses so I asked the steward to put a £5 bet on the horse for me. He did, it lost, and so did I. In those days £5 was quite a lot of money but at least the overtime covered my loss.

THE CAR SQUAD

In February 1970 I was appointed detective sergeant and took charge of the Motor Vehicle Investigation Squad, better known as the Car Squad.

I had three squads based at Cumnor just outside Oxford, Bracknell and Aylesbury. Despite obvious bias I can claim the Car Squad was highly successful and we recovered well over £1,000,000 worth of stolen property each year.

Our terms of reference were fairly loose, as long as we recovered stolen property and arrested criminals; we were to a large extent left alone to do our own thing.

We came under the supervision of the detective inspector in charge of Scenes of Crime Department for administrative purposes and ultimately under the assistant chief constable (Crime.)

We dealt with practically every form of transport and mechanical devices, cars, lorries, motorcycles, industrial and contractor's plant, farm equipment, boats, caravans, in fact everything that has an engine and/or wheels, except skateboards and pedal cycles.

Each of my officers developed a good working

knowledge of all these different modes of transport then most of the squad specialised in particular topics, for instance, I became an expert in insurance fraud and auto arson, one of my men was an expert on motorcycles, another on heavy goods vehicles, and so on.

To support our growing knowledge we collected and catalogued a huge amount of information on our specialist subjects to such an extent that other forces, knowing this vast pool of information was available would use us as a sort of information centre.

Occasionally, we were called upon to work on other enquiries such as murders, rapes and explosions where vehicles were involved.

Any vehicle enquiry from Interpol was directed to our offices. We were in a way the liaison between the Thames Valley Police and the Driver and Vehicle Licensing Centre, Swansea and advised them on any unusual vehicle or circumstance.

In time we became a well informed and very experienced squad.

A SURPRISING QUICK FLIP

I was asked to interview a sergeant in the Royal Air Force at RAF, Bicester about a stolen car that he had inadvertently purchased.

I was in the process of taking a statement when he asked me if I had ever been in a glider. I said I had not, then without further preamble he got up and said,

"Follow me."

Within minutes we were airborne. He took me up in a Volkswagen powered glider to about 3,500 feet then shut off the engine, it was quite eerie but exhilarating.

I recall we went over a car park in Bicester where the heat reflecting off the roofs of the parked cars on that hot sunny day gave us about a 500 foot lift.

The RAF sergeant was one of the country's top glider pilots who took part in acrobatic competitions so I was in good hands. I am glad he did not do any acrobatics whilst I was with him.

This was quite an unexpected and very enjoyable trip and inspired by this experience, later I took gliding lessons but the gliding school was to put it bluntly a shambles, after a few lessons I gave up and therefore did not gain my glider pilot's licence.

THE DOWDY DAMSEL

In 1971 I spent three months in London attending a Senior CID course held at the Metropolitan Police Training School, Hendon.

There were about twenty five male students on this course including several from overseas and from the Military Police, plus one female, a detective sergeant from the Devon and Cornwall Police.

I will use the expression dowdy to describe this female with good reason. Aged about 35 years she wore brogue shoes, thick woollen stockings, a drab woollen costume and her hair, unbelievably, was done up in a bun. She was the most unattractive female imaginable.

At the end of the three month course we had a dinner dance, an event we all dressed up for. When this lady entered the room everyone, and I mean everyone, was stunned. Wearing makeup, a revealing black evening dress, high heels and her hair done up in a most attractive style, she was a stunner, a real beauty with a fantastic figure.

During the course of that social event she was the centre of attention. It was interesting, even amusing to see the reactions of some of those sex starved men as they lusted after her. From an ugly duckling she had morphed into an elegant swan.

Reflecting on this transformation I believe she deliberately made herself unattractive to deter men pestering her whilst on this long and intensive course. If so, good for her.

LADYBIRD GARAGE

When I lectured at the Police Training Centre in Sulhamstead one aspect I always dwelt on was that the car thief could be so good in disguising a car that many unwary buyers had been conned into buying a stolen car, and even police officers have fallen into this trap.

Then one of the audience piped up that he had a car that he knew was not stolen because he had bought it new from a main dealership. How wrong could he be!

One of the first enquiries I dealt with when I joined the Car Squad was the theft of three brand new Minis from the factory in Cowley, Oxford.

In the early 1970's production was in full swing at Cowley manufacturing the Morris Mini. These cars were delivered to the Morris Dealerships throughout the country by a contracted car transporter firm.

The usual procedure was that the transporter lorries were loaded up during the late afternoon, four cars on the lower deck and three on the upper deck, ready for the next day's deliveries. Those on the lower deck were locked and keys removed but those on the upper deck were not so secured and the keys were left in the ignition. Who could steal a car that was ten feet up in the air?

Late one afternoon one of the transporter drivers loaded up his lorry and then, instead of parking it with the other lorries he drove it to the other end of this huge secure lorry park and reversed it up to and touching a seven foot high wire fence and left it there.

This driver was at work earlier than normal, collected his lorry whilst no one was about and parked it where it should have been, with the others, and went away for a time.

Then shortly afterwards he returned to the car park and to his, and the other driver's amazement found all three cars that were on the upper deck were missing. It was a total surprise.

When I arrived at my office at 9am that morning the telephone was already ringing, it was the car plant Security Officer reporting the theft of the three Minis. By 9:20am Jock and I were at the plant and commencing our enquiries.

Jock interviewed the driver who professed he was innocent as the day is long; meanwhile I interviewed the other drivers. One of them told me that he had seen the lorry in question with a full load of minis being driven to the other side of the car park late the previous afternoon.

We walked across to where he had seen it parked and I saw on the other side of the wire fence there was an area of waste ground and clearly marked on the soft ground were the tyre impressions made by a heavy lorry. I had got the picture.

During the night another car transporter had arrived and the driver had driven onto the waste ground, reversed up to the fence directly opposite the one with the Minis so the lorries were back to back and the top decks touching and then the three mini's had simply been driven from one transporter over the wire fence onto the other transporter. This was a very simple and effective operation.

I returned to the office where Jock was still taking a statement, I whispered to Jock what I had found out, he then said to the driver

"How much did you get for reversing up to the perimeter fence last night so the Minis could be driven over the fence onto another transporter?"

He realised the game was up and changed his story and made a statement of admission.

He admitted he had indeed received money from the director of a garage in Leicester to park in such a manner so the Minis could be off-loaded, £200 per car.

By 12:30pm that day Jock and I were at Ladybird Garage in Leicester where we interviewed one of the directors. He did not deny his involvement in the theft; he couldn't have, as we had found all three stolen cars on his premises.

The driver, director and the driver of the other car transporter were arrested, charged and convicted. All three Minis were returned to the factory, still in brand new condition.

Not bad for one day's work and the Morris Factory management were highly delighted at the prompt and very successful result of the enquiry.

If we had not twigged on what had happened all three

new Minis would have been sold on to innocent purchasers.

A DAY IN COURT

I was in the Crown Court whilst one of my cases was being heard when the Judge said that he would retire for a short break. The constable on duty, in the absence of the court usher, called "All rise."

Everyone in the Court stood except for a detective inspector. When the constable glared at him the detective inspector went to the constable and gave him a ticking off, saying, "I do not stand on the order of a mere constable." Needless to say the constable felt chastised.

When the Judge returned the constable called out, "All rise," and again the detective inspector remained seated

When the Court adjourned for lunch I went over to the detective inspector and told him that in the absence of the Court Usher the constable was acting correctly and he, the detective inspector, was out of order by not standing. He nearly blew his top and as he started to say he would not take any notice of what

I was saying, the superintendent, who had entered the court and heard the gist of the argument, gave the detective inspector a right rollicking telling him that he was lucky he was not to be charged with contempt of court. That shut him up.

I noticed later that afternoon he stood, somewhat slowly when the words "all rise" were called out. He was an ignorant so and so.

THE CITY OF MILTON KEYNES

During 1960/1970's, work commenced on the building of the new City of Milton Keynes. This was a huge project covering several square miles of building houses, factories, leisure complexes and shops for a quarter of a million people. This meant there was an awful lot of construction equipment working on these building sites.

Soon after I joined the Car Squad in 1970 I was appointed the Police Plant Liaison Officer to the Milton Keynes Development Corporation and in this role I attended numerous planning meetings to advise on security matters and give updates on reported crimes.

At one of the meetings I reported an increase in the number of thefts of plant equipment, especially of JCB diggers. I advised that the Oxford and Aylesbury Car Squads were paying particular attention to this specific problem.

Resulting from these enquiries our investigations led us to a certain Irishman called Mr Finn.

Mr Finn used three legitimately purchased JCB diggers on a contract to dig the footings for new houses. He also had a plant hire business and this was the side of the business we were interested in.

Our observations were to bear fruit and we learnt that his nice little earner of a scam was simple but effective. After the other contractors had finished work for the day Mr Finn would drive his low loader lorry onto the site, steal any JBC he could find by winching it onto the low loader, take it to his yard in Northampton where he would remove the number plates, mutilate the chassis number and then paint the JCB a sickly yellowy/green colour.

Apparently he had purchased a bulk lot of ex-service khaki paint that he mixed with some spare yellow paint producing a colour we called Finn Green.

Within hours of theft the JCB was adorned with this new colour. He would then advertise the JCB for hire.

With enough evidence obtained we visited Mr Finn at his Northampton depot, confronted him with the evidence and he readily admitted his involvement so he was arrested and charged.

In one of the charges we brought against him Finn had stolen a JCB from a contractor in Milton Keynes and carried out its disguise. The contractor arrived at work the very next day to find his JCB had been stolen and faced with the problem of fulfilling the contract, contacted Finn Plant Hire of Northampton to hire a replacement JCB until his insurance claim was met. Mr Finn hired him a JCB, which our enquiries showed was his (the contractors) own machine that had been stolen from him the previous night. What a cheek.

Our enquiries revealed that Finn's entire fleet of hired plant consisted of stolen items.

In fairness to Mr Finn, after his arrest he was most cooperative and took us round the sites at Milton Keynes and elsewhere pointing out items of property he had stolen. He seemed quite proud of his achievements. In all, during this one enquiry we recovered just under £1,000,000 worth of stolen property.

Despite his later help Mr Finn went to prison and his business was wound up.

Yes, my squad earned our keep and we kept the Milton Keynes Development Corporation very happy.

ODE TO AN IRISHMAN

There was an Irishman named Finn,
Whose face bore a great big grin,
Why was he so pleased?
Why, he had stolen some JCB'S.

Alas, his glee was not to last,
The Car Squad were on a blast,
His criminal acts were to no avail,
Those sneaky coppers were on his trail.

His Finn green paint, a ghastly hue,
Was the revealing clue,
At last we had him licked,
As we uttered those immortal words,
"You're nicked."

IAATI

In August 1979 I went to the United States of America to attend an Auto Crime Seminar at Denver, Colorado being run by the International Association of Auto Theft Investigators.

It all came about when I was walking along Oxford Road, Cowley, and in the window of a travel agent there was a large replica of the Boeing 747 jumbo jet. Now, I had never been in a jumbo jet, or to America, so there and then I went in and booked a flight to Denver. This on the spot decision vastly altered my life.

At Denver I met so many nice people, mainly police officers, who were to become my wife and my closest friends. I joined IAATI; I believe I was the third police officer from Europe to become a member.

Later I was made a Director of the Association, and then in the 1989 I formed the European Branch of this association and was elected its first President. Why didn't I keep my head down? I am always being talked into organising things or taking up committee positions.

It was my own fault because in 1984 I had organised a

four day Auto Crime Seminar at Heathrow, and then in 1987 a further four day seminar at Leicester Polytechnic, both well attended and successful.

The 1984 seminar was the first ever International Autocrime Seminar to be held in Europe.

At the 1987 Seminar we had delegates from Australia, South Africa, Israel, Japan, practically every country in Europe, including Russia, and two delegates even came all the way from Alaska.

THE CHP PATROL CAR

My office was on Cumnor Hill just outside Oxford in what were originally three houses. Two, the outside ones, were still police houses but the middle one had been converted into offices. My squad had two downstairs rooms; the dog section sergeant occupied the third. Upstairs were the offices of the secretary and the civilian force welfare officer.

On a trip to the United States my friend Gene who was then in the California Highway Patrol had given me a couple of their car logos that were used on the sides of their patrol cars. I decided to make my police car like one of theirs.

In 1979 my police car was a plain white Morris Marina, the only police equipment was a radio installed inside the glove compartment.

Arriving early at my office I had something to do. Just for a joke I fitted to both front doors of the police Marina these huge peel–off door size California Highway Patrol logos.

I went into the office and looked out of the window hoping to see the reactions of my men when they arrived for work, but to my horror, a car pulled up and two superintendents from the Forces Complaints and Discipline Department alighted, looked at my police car, walked around it a couple of times, had a discussion and then made for the offices. I was frantically trying to think of an excuse, but to my relief they made their way upstairs to the welfare office.

For the next couple of hours I was on tenterhooks wondering if they would see me on their way out but after completing their meeting they made their way downstairs and drove off. As their car left the premises I was outside like a shot and peeled off those logos - just in case.

AIR BAGS

Dwight is another friend who was in the California Highway Patrol and in 1985 he took me to the California Highway Patrol office in Sacramento to attend an Air Bag Seminar. This was something new to me as the theft of air bags was then unheard of in England. The theft of air bags in America, particularly in the state of California is so widespread that special squads had been set up to deal with the problem and this seminar was to discuss the current situation.

Imagine a minor accident involving two cars. At the speed of about 15 to 20 miles per hour the air bags would be activated. The damage to the car itself would be minimal, say costing 250 dollars to repair, but to replace the two front air bags would cost between 1,000 and 1,500 dollars each, in other words these items would now contribute to the major cost of repair in a minor to a moderately severe accident.

Air bag thieves steal cars specifically to remove the air bags and sell them to unscrupulous car repairers for about 250 to 300 dollars each and then the repairer would charge his customer the full cost of replacement with the owner believing the car had been fitted with new air bags. A very lucrative trade all round.

Air bags, or to be more specific, the removal of air bags serve another purpose. When removed the space previously occupied in the steering wheel boss and in front of the passenger seat by the air bags is utilised for the carriage of drugs, contraband and firearms.

Unless the police or customs officers were aware of this possibility then it is an almost foolproof method of moving contraband from state to state, or country to country.

Up to when I retired from the police in September 1986 I had not come across any of the above mentioned criminal practices in the UK.

SOLDIERS AND A LAND ROVER

My two lads (John & Bob) at Aylesbury came across another nice little earner thought out by a squaddie stationed in Germany.

He stole a Land Rover from the Aylesbury area, drove it to Germany where he presented it to the appropriate Army Department together with a forged purchase receipt.

The Army Authorities, under the British Forces Germany regulations, issued him with the BOAR registration plates and a registration document.

Six months later the squaddie, taking two weeks leave, returned to England, presented the Land Rover and the BOAR registration document to the local Vehicle Taxation Office and received a UK registration document in exchange. He now had a stolen vehicle on legitimate plates and registration document, which he was able to sell for a very good price.

A few months later the squaddie and another soldier stole two more vehicles that they took to Germany, no doubt to continue this profitable scam, but John and Bob were up to speed and an all-expenses paid trip was made to Germany and the two were arrested and both vehicles recovered. The squaddies were later convicted.

Somewhat belatedly after this the Army tightened up the system for the registration of cars overseas.

THE AMERSHAM BAKER

When a police officer asked for my help in dealing with a road accident I was inclined to say no, that was not my job but when he said an insurance fraud may be involved I changed my mind.

A baker who lived in Amersham used to leave his home and family at 9pm each evening to go to work, and returned home about 6am the next morning but it appears he did not go straight to work as he firstly visited his fancy woman and stayed with her until midnight and then went on to work.

One evening he asked his fancy woman to go out and get some fish and chips and handed her his car keys. Twenty minutes later on a bend she crashed the car into another vehicle. She sustained moderate injuries and the car was badly damaged. The two occupants of the other car were not injured.

When later interviewed by a police officer the baker claimed he was the driver and after the crash he ran away from the scene. The occupants of the other car strongly insisted a woman was driving.

An Insurance Investigator later interviewed the baker and he insisted to him as well that he was the driver.

There was no doubt that the fancy woman was not insured and it was thought he was trying to keep her out of trouble.

At this point I was asked to interview the baker, no doubt hoping that I may bring further pressure to bear on the man, but he still stoutly claimed he was the driver and I took a statement from him to this effect.

I had had enough of his lies so I tried a different tack. From the information he provided in his statement I typed onto a Criminal Justice statement form a Statutory Declaration:

I (his name) declare I am the registered owner of the car number (registration number).

I (his name) declare at (time) on the (date) at (place) I was the driver when it was involved in an accident.

I (his name) declare that at no time has Miss (fancy woman's name) driven my car.

and other pertinent items of information.

I telephoned the baker and told him that the following Tuesday he would be required to attend the office of a Commissioner for Oaths in Amersham and sign the Statutory Declaration. I advised him that if he signed the declaration knowing the information contained therein was false it would be akin to giving false evidence on oath in a court of law and the penalty would be the same as for perjury, a penalty of a maximum of seven years imprisonment.

That must have frightened him as the next day I received a telephone call from a solicitor advising me that his client, the baker, wished to change his statement as he now admitted his fancy lady was, after all, the driver of the car.

Now, apparently it was not the fear of a conviction for permitting uninsured use of his car that was the reason for his previous lies, it was the fear that his wife would find out what he had been doing between 9pm and 12 midnight, five days a week. She must have been a formidable woman. He was eventually convicted.

TRAVELLER ENCAMPMENTS

Most people will be aware that some Traveller encampments are a no-go area for the police, and to a certain extent I can understand this, as anyone who is reasonably dressed would be treated with hostility. Even those sites with a Traveller Warden are little better.

On several occasions during my sixteen years with the Car Squad we, together with the Support Group, local police and occasionally with the Firearms Unit have executed warrants at these encampments and to be truthful this heavy handed approach is probably the best way to deal with those who may have been involved in criminal activities and lived on these sites.

There is no need to expand on the problems with these encampments, as there has been plenty of media attention to these mostly illegal sites over the past few years.

As could be expected, after I left the Police and became an Insurance Investigator, I had to, on my own to visit these sites and was almost always met with hostility but I found a simple solution.

Travellers know the law and they also know how to extract money from the Local Authorities and the insurance companies and I have dealt with many Traveller insurance claims.

Usually as I drove onto a Traveller site a gang of hostile kids would surround the car, all the women would go into the caravans and the men would stand around looking aggressive. I would pick out one man, go up to him and say I was looking for, say Samuel Loveridge, of course, the Traveller thinking I was either a police officer or a local council official would say that no one of that name lived on the site.

I would then say that his insurance company would be pleased because if I cannot find him then the insurance company will not have to make an insurance payment. It's amazing how quickly the man I wanted appeared and the cooperation I received.

Then I had to do a bit of bargaining. I would tell him that if he did not put a guard on my car, any damage caused to it would be deducted from his insurance claim. That worked as well.

It might be considered unfair to paint Travellers in a bad light, in other words, treat them with the utmost suspicion, but on the other hand these types of people are the most suspicious persons I have met in my thirty years in the police and fifteen years as an insurance investigator. Their suspicious nature often borders on aggression.

BORDER CONFERENCES

Other duties permitting, every Wednesday one of my colleagues and I would visit the Motor Auctions held near Frimley, Surrey. The location of the auction is on the borders of Hampshire and the Thames Valley.

Prior to the auction starting we would check out the

vehicles waiting to be auctioned. Due to the large numbers involved only cursory checks could be made. Looking for new plates, plates held on by new screws, signs of the chassis plates being tampered with and alterations made to the tax disc, etc.

There we would meet up with Peter, the Hampshire Car Squad man and after the auction was over we would retire to the local hostelry for a bite to eat and a chat. This was the time for the interchange of information about our mutual interest – stolen vehicles.

Later Ron and Dave from the Surrey Car Squad joined us at the auctions. It was then I realised that these informal meetings were vital for the exchange of information. Car thieves have no respect for boundaries so I decided to put these informal meetings on a more structured basis and to widen its scope.

I arranged an evening meeting at Bracknell Police Station. Car Squad officers from above mentioned forces plus representatives from the Metropolitan, Kent, Wiltshire and Sussex Police were invited. Then at later meetings we incorporated officers from the Avon and Somerset and Essex police. The Border Conferences were born.

The first hour was designated for either a formal interchange of information or a talk by a representative from other interested parties such as the motor manufacturers, the DVLA, the insurance industry, motor auctions, etc.

Then we retired to the bar where the host force would supply light refreshments, and this is where little groups got together and the swapping of really valuable information proved most fruitful.

I was appointed Chairman of the Border Conference for the first year, and these three monthly meetings, held in different force area proved to be well worthwhile, in fact we had requests from forces as far away as Huntingdonshire and Leicestershire for their car squad members to be represented.

The previously mentioned Ron of the Surrey Car Squad was a valuable addition to the meeting; he was a first class thief-taker with excellent contacts in the underworld. In fact he had so many grasses (informants) that if they were all put together they would make a sizeable lawn!

We used to call these sources of information grasses, snouts, narks, informants, but no more; according to police instructions they now have to be referred to as CHIS – Covert Human Intelligence Sources. I wonder who thought up this brilliant idea!

When I retired in 1986, the Border Conference members presented me with a wine decanter and six wine glasses, each glass had been engraved with the crest of the original six forces that made up the Border Conference. This was a very nice present that I cherish but they are only used on special occasions.

THE CAR AUCTIONS

When checking cars at the auctions we had to act as if we were prospective buyers just in case the seller-cum-thief was hovering about. We would check the usual things, the speedo reading, kick the tyres, check the spare wheel, check the bodywork for dents, etc.

If we located a suspect car we would have a word with the auction's chief security officer, who was very pro-police probably because he was a retired chief superintendent from the Metropolitan Police.

We would use his phone to check with the Police National Computer to confirm that the car was indeed stolen. The CSO would have a word with the auctioneer, no, not to have the car removed from the auction but to let it run through.

The auctioneer would accept bids on the suspect car from the punters but would also accept bids from a 'ghost' punter and of course the car would be knocked down to the ghost punter.

The purchase and sales office at the auction was a very busy place with potentially a seller and a buyer for the five hundred or so cars up for sale on each sale day. After the sale of the stolen car had gone through the seller-cum-thief would make tracks to this office where he hoped to come away with a sheaf of bank notes, and where we would be keeping a discreet watch. Once he had filled out the paperwork in relation to the supposed sale made by him, we would swoop and carry out the arrest and the confiscation of the car.

This procedure was developed into a fine art over the months; it became a sort of routine and a very satisfactory routine at that.

THE POLICE NATIONAL COMPUTER

The Police National Computer (PNC) was introduced in the early 1970's and teams of civil servants from the Home Office toured the country, visiting Police Stations and giving advice to selected police officers about its operations. As an officer dealing with stolen vehicles I was one of those selected to meet these

Home Office boffins.

I recall one of them telling me that once up and running there would be no need of a Stolen Car Squad as every police officer would have access to the PNC and by providing the registration number, chassis number (as it was then) and/or engine number they could ascertain within seconds whether or not the vehicle was stolen.

How wrong they were and how ill-advised they appeared to be, as they were unaware that the professional car thief would change the registration and the chassis plates to thwart the PNC records. But my initial worry that I would lose my squads was soon allayed as autocrime went up and the recovery rate went down. Why?

Well, the answer is simple. The PNC was God and if the PNC said a vehicle was not stolen then that was gospel, it was not stolen.

Prior to the PNC coming into operation if an officer's suspicion was aroused to the extent he would check out a car, he would question the driver and if necessary detain him/her, but with the PNC in operation if the computer said a vehicle was not stolen then that was it, the driver was allowed to go, even if the car was stolen.

I have known of officers who would occasionally

check a suspect car's identity without even stopping it.

A simple example comes to mind. A commuter leaves his car at a railway station car park at 8am, locks it up and takes the keys with him. At 10am the car is broken into and stolen. At 10:30am the thief driving the car is stopped by police, the registration number checked on the PNC and it comes back as not stolen; the thief is allowed to drive away.

The reason it was not recorded stolen was simply because the driver, busy at work did not know and would not know until he returned to the car park at the end of the working day that his car had been stolen. Hence no stolen report on the PNC.

I could relate many instances of a similar nature when this has happened but I am sure my readers will have got the picture.

One of the most important factors I mentioned at the lectures I gave at the Force Training School was the cautious necessity of not believing the computer if the officer's suspicions had been roused about the driver and/or car.

Despite my reservations about its efficiency and usefulness I believe the PNC was and still is a vital tool in the fight against all types of crime and on many occasions I have been grateful for the rapid and successful response it has provided me with, particularly when multiple searches of stolen vehicle records have been necessary.

ANPR

At the seminar I organised at Leicester Polytechnic in 1987 one of the items on the agenda was a display by the Home Office of a new piece of equipment called the ANPR (Automatic Number Plate Reader).

This device, connected to the Police National Computer read the number plate of passing vehicles, checked it with the database of stolen vehicles and if stolen this information would be available to the police within seconds.

The delivery of this device to the police was eagerly awaited; I knew my squad would be very happy to site it in some of the stolen car black spots in our towns and cities.

Alas, the Home Office decreed that it was too expensive to bring into use and all that research was wasted. However, I do know that some years after I retired from the police, the ANPR was in police use and by then it had been enhanced to include disqualified drivers, uninsured, untaxed and vehicles suspected to be used in crimes and suspect terrorists.

The ANPR is also sited at the docks and at the entrance to the Eurotunnel in Folkestone to check on vehicles arriving and leaving the country. How I wish we could have used them when I was a serving officer.

Since September 2014 when the issue of the Vehicle Excise Licence came to an end, the ANPR has assumed a more important role. Literally thousands of ANPR cameras have, and are still being installed, on all major roads to detect not only untaxed vehicles but also those uninsured, those that have not been currently MOT tested and for other motoring offences.

DVLC.

The Driver and Vehicle Licensing Centre, (DVLC) as it was then called, and based at Morriston, Swansea, started to computerise the motor vehicle records in 1970 and to this end the 43 Local Taxation Offices in England, Scotland and Wales extracted from the manual files of each vehicle registered with them, two documents.

The first was the vehicle's original application form to register the vehicle. This document contained the vehicle specification, engine and chassis number, make, model, colour, date of first registration, first owner and of course the registration number allocated. The second document required was that of the last registered keeper.

From this information a computer record of the vehicle was set up and the new registration document was generated and sent to the last registered keeper.

Any motorist who owned a vehicle at the time of this transition must be aware that an awful lot of the new vehicle registration documents contained errors. A motorist with a Morris Minor may find his new registration document showed it as a road roller, etc.

Needless to say a lot of these errors were brought to my attention and I took up the problems with the DVLC. The upshot was that I was invited to Swansea to see the cause of the problem.

With some fifteen million vehicle registrations to be processed it was inevitable there would be some mistakes, but I was deeply impressed by the set up at Swansea.

With about two hundred ladies processing the documents, they were split up into teams of twelve, and two in each team worked together with linked computers. One would enter the data from the paperwork into her computer and hand the file to the second who would do the same. If the information on both computers did not correspond then the entry would be rejected and it would then be looked at more closely. Added to this, each supervisor of the team of twelve would triple check about every twentieth file.

So how did the errors occur? The mistakes as a general rule were not the fault of the DVLC staff but were made when the supplying dealer first registered the car.

In those days the majority of applications to register a new car were handwritten by either a salesman or a clerk at the supplying garage and due care was not always taken.

For instance the chassis number of a 1970 Ford Cortina started with the digits BB. I have seen several of these applications with these two digits reading 1313. And a 5 may appear as an S and an E as an F. The mistakes in almost every case were badly written applications.

As regards the names and addresses transcribed from the old written records onto the computer, well, the mistakes were numerous and in some cases rather amusing.

With the list of some fifty queries that I took to the DVLC almost all of them were due to errors of the type described above, and not the fault of the ladies at the DVLC.

Typical errors that appeared on registration documents were vehicles given the wrong classification, wrong engine size or even shown as the wrong model.

THE VOLVO

One scheme devised by the DVLC, the insurance industry and the police was the monitoring of motor vehicles that had been written off in accidents, stolen, burnt out or of interest to the police or insurance industry in that the vehicle may have been the subject of crime.

To this end the DVLC sent to my office on average thirty of these enquiries a week. These enquiries known as VQ13's were monitored by me and where there was an element of suspicion I would pass the enquiry on to one of my men for further enquiries.

One such VQ13 enquiry related to a nearly new Volvo car that had been written off in an accident having sustained severe body damage. The trigger to my interest was that the date between the salvage being sold to a garage by the insurance company and being registered, taxed and insured by the new owner was only two weeks. No way could a car with the damage described on the accident report be repaired, sold and registered within two weeks. It was time for further enquiries.

I telephoned the previous and first owner, the car was less than a year old and he told me that in his opinion the car was only lightly damaged and he was surprised that the insurance company had written it off. He was not too perturbed though as they had supplied him with a new car.

As the new owner of the Volvo I was interested in lived on the outskirts of Reading and only a mile or so from the Training Centre at Sulhamstead where I lectured at least once a week, I decided I would deal with this particular enquiry.

I must have gone past the new owner's house at least a dozen times, then one afternoon the Volvo was in the driveway of the bungalow and an elderly gentleman was mowing the front lawn.

After introducing myself I told the new owner that I proposed to examine his Volvo, he then became very agitated, I ignored him, he then tried to be aggressive but not with much success. As I commenced my in depth examination looking for signs of damage repair he must have seen me shaking my head and making copious notes, as he broke down and started to cry.

I believe he saw that the insurance assessor's examination form I was referring to was the one he had made out in respect of the Volvo.

At my request we went into his bungalow where I suggested he had better tell me what the true story was. Well, it was a surprise as I had expected to find the car was stolen, a cut and shut, or it had been obtained by fraud, and in fact the latter was the case.

The man told me that for forty years he had been an insurance assessor working diligently for one of the major insurance companies and during the years he had come across hundreds of cases where both customers of the insurance companies, garages and freelance motor dealers had ripped off the insurance companies whilst dealing with crashed vehicles.

As he approached retirement he felt that to supplement his measly pension he should also have a bonus and if his employers would not give him a decent bonus he would take one himself.

When he received the paperwork to examine the above mentioned Volvo at the garage of a breakdown company, it was a top of the range model; he decided that this car would serve him well. The Volvo, as the previous owner had told me, had been accident damaged but the damage was not substantial and could probably be repaired for less than £1,000.

The insurance assessor reported to his employer, the insurance company, that the car had sustained severe damage to the underside and the cost to put it right would be several thousands of pounds. The insurance company wrote it off and supplied the first owner with a new car. They then sold the alleged wrecked car to the garage for £800.

The former insurance assessor had colluded with the breakdown garage owner to defraud the insurance company.

The garage owner got his cut; about £1,000 for repairing the car, the insurance assessor had obtained a nearly new car for about £1,800. Quite a bargain.

Now I had to deal with the insurance assessor. He was in a sorry state, the first crime he had ever committed and had been found out, I arrested him and subsequently he was convicted of criminal deception. That man, greatly respected in his community with an impeccable reputation for over forty years now had a criminal record.

THE TRIKE

When, in the early 1970's the DVLC received a letter from a member of the public requesting advice on how to register a vehicle he had built, the DVLC sent the letter to the Police Headquarters at Kidlington and as expected, anything difficult and of a motoring nature ended up on my desk.

About two miles from the small village of Milton in Oxfordshire there is an isolated farm and the farmer rented out a barn to this enterprising young man who had built an unusual motor vehicle.

This young man had grafted together the rear end of a Volkswagen Beetle car to the front of a Kawasaki motorcycle. This may seem a somewhat crude creation but he had created a masterpiece.

To match the two vastly different vehicles together he had to fashion quite a large number of specialist parts and these, carefully crafted and chromed were like pieces of art in themselves. During my years on the Car Squad I had examined hundreds of vehicles but this one stood out as the most impressive.

The problem was identification and classification. What was it, a car or a bike, or a tricycle? An in-depth examination was called for. To be classified as a three-wheeler it had to, in those days, weigh less than 8 hundredweight and comply with certain conditions. If under 8 cwt it did not require a reverse gear. However this vehicle did have a gearbox, with a reverse gear.

Did the vehicle require Type Approval? Did it comply with the Construction and Use Regulations? What was its year of manufacture? The car part and the motorcycle part were made in different years? Was it in a roadworthy condition? As it was half motorcycle and half car would the rider/driver be required to wear a safety (crash) helmet and/or wear a seat belt?

The problems did not end there; the front half bore a motorcycle frame/VIN number and the rear half bore a car engine number.

Another problem, what colour should be entered on the registration document? It had been sprayed to a very high order in psychedelic colours and there was no predominant colour and I am sure the DVLC would not be happy with 'multi.'

After a detailed examination I was able to make certain recommendations. The identifying features were erased from the headstock and engine and new numbers of the 'International Standards Organisation' format stamped onto the frame and engine. I suggested that as most of the parts of the vehicle were 'used' it should be supplied with a 'Q' registration number. I recommended that if possible seat belts were fitted and the rider be required to wear a safety helmet.

Neither of these last two suggestions were taken up but it is my belief that the rider, in any case, for his own safety should wear a helmet. If he chose not to and was involved in an accident in which he sustained head injuries almost certainly an insurance company would use this for a reason to decline or greatly reduce a claim for his injuries.

After being weighed and MOT tested the machine was registered and later used on the road. This was much to the relief of the owner who had devoted many hundreds of hours in its construction.

There is an unhappy postscript to this young man's endeavours. His next project was the construction of a tricycle using a SAAB two stroke three cylinder engine and gearbox, and the front of a motorcycle. I saw this machine as it was almost ready for use on the road, then one evening the barn he rented, containing this tricycle, was burnt down and the machine destroyed.

AUTO ARSON EXPERTISE

My expertise in auto arson came about in bits and pieces. During the early 1980's an American colleague, Lee Cole who was the foremost auto arson expert in the United States, came to England to holiday with my wife and I. Lee had been invited to attend an Auto Arson Seminar organised by the London Fire Brigade and I was invited to join them. I learnt a lot that day.

The International Association of Auto Theft Investigators holds a seminar in the United States each year and auto arson always features on the programme.

Over the years I was with the Stolen Car Squad I had attended some twelve of these seminars and these arson lectures considerably forwarded my knowledge in this topic.

Then add to that the knowledge I had gained from the examination of literally hundreds of burnt out vehicles, I believe I can now claim a certain expertise.

In 1984 I gave a lecture at an Auto Theft Conference at Heathrow on this subject, and arising from this I was asked to go to Pretoria, South Africa, all-expenses paid, to lecture to the South African Police, so I must have been saying the right things at the Heathrow Conference.

When Major Willem Smith picked up my wife and me at Johannesburg airport he was driving a late model BMW. I commented on this and Willem explained that when they seized a stolen or suspect vehicle the police, if the owner could not be traced, they commandeered the vehicle for their own use. He further explained that if the stolen vehicle was a good one, the police did not try very hard to identify it or trace the owner. I noted that quite a number of high ranking police officers were using expensive cars. No doubt that helped with their police budget!

THE STOLEN PEDAL CYCLE

The car squad did not investigate pedal cycle thefts but when a constable at Bicester asked me to investigate a report of a stolen cycle involving a forged receipt I agreed as I had developed a reasonable ability to detect forged papers. The receipt for the purchase of a new cycle had obviously been altered.

The person who reported the cycle stolen was a soldier stationed at the army barracks just outside Bicester so I made arrangements to see him.

When confronted with the doctored receipt he readily agreed that he had altered it by erasing his friend's name and inserting his own. He told me that he and his friend had bought identical cycles on the same day, for the same price and from the same cycle dealer.

When he reported its theft to his insurance company they wanted to see the purchase receipt for his cycle but he could not find it so he borrowed his friend's receipt and changed their names. Yes, he had forged the receipt. The receipt was then for some reason sent to Bicester police by the insurance company.

I saw the other soldier and he confirmed he had loaned his receipt to his friend, he also confirmed his friend's cycle had been stolen. This seemed a reasonable explanation but to tidy up the enquiry I visited the cycle shop in Bicester and the owner confirmed both soldiers had bought identical cycles on the same day and for the same price.

The cycle dealer told me that if the problem had been brought to his attention he would have issued a replacement receipt.

Taking into account no criminal act with intent to

defraud had been committed I decided no further action should be taken against the soldier, and I am pleased to say that the insurance company dealing with the claim, despite the fact the soldier had done a stupid thing, shared my view and the soldier received payment for the loss of his cycle.

THE EGYPTIAN MILLIONAIRE

Probably the most spectacular crime I have helped with occurred in Reading. It was there that an Egyptian millionaire purchased a disused office building, converted it into flats and he was making a very good profit from the rent of the flats as they were in a prime location.

When another disused office building nearby came on the market, the Egyptian's brother decided to get in on the act and he purchased this building with a view to conversion. Alas, his application to turn the offices into flats was turned down, as it was unknown to him at the time, a listed building.

He was left with an unwanted building so to recoup his loss he made contact with a well-known and notorious London criminal, formerly an associate of the Kray's and Richardson's, who agreed for a fee to set fire to the building so the Egyptian could make an insurance claim.

Late at night the criminal entered the building with four cans of petrol and starting on the top (third) floor sprinkled a gallon of petrol onto each floor. On the ground floor, exercising what he thought was care he sprinkled the petrol from the last can from the back of the building to the front. Near the front door he lit a match. The whole place exploded. He achieved his aim but in doing so killed himself.

My involvement came about because of the experience I had gained in auto arson and for some reason a senior officer thought this experience would be good in the investigation of an office fire.

I attended the criminal's inquest and the pathologist gave evidence that the dead man had inhaled so much of the petrol fumes that in the explosion his lungs were literally incinerated.

A week or so later I interviewed the widow of the dead man at her home in London. She was a brassy and rough looking lady who apparently associated with some of the top London criminals. She did not appear to be in mourning for the loss of her husband; I think she was happy that he had blown himself up.

She readily admitted that her husband had previously

told her that he was being paid by the Egyptian to set the place alight. He was going to receive £5,000 for the cost of four gallons of petrol.

It was whilst I was talking to the widow that three tough looking characters entered the house through the back door and demanded in a threatening manner what my interest was. I was not prepared to tell them and demanded to know what they wanted. After a standoff for about ten minutes they eventually told me they were Metropolitan police officers and the lady was one of their best informants. That eased the tension and the meeting ended on an amicable note.

I was worried, no, very worried for a time as I thought that those three men may have been associates of the Kray's or Richardson's.

I worked the investigation with a very experienced Fire Investigation Officer from the local Fire Brigade and sufficient evidence was produced to charge the Egyptian for attempted insurance fraud and an arrest warrant in his name was taken out.

Needless to say the insurance claim was rejected and the Egyptian, to evade prosecution hotfooted it out of the country. As far as I am aware the warrant is still outstanding.

One very sad side issue is that when one of the windows was blown out in the blast, a concrete lintel was blown across the street and hit a young lad who was seriously injured leaving him permanently paralysed.

Fortunately, he was able to claim compensation from the Egyptian's insurance company.

THE BLACK MINI

When a police officer goes on duty he has no idea what the day is going to throw at him, where he will end the day and who he might meet. During a very cold spell in November I met up with a very unsavoury character under circumstances that could have turned extremely nasty.

A brand new and unregistered Mini had been stolen overnight from a car compound just outside Reading. The perimeter fence to the compound had been cut open and the car taken away by a transporter.

The thief made a big mistake, the car, a special order, was all black and this was a very unusual colour for a Mini, so I was not surprised when, in response to my circulations I received information that a new black Mini had been registered with Berkshire County Council Taxation Department.

I interviewed the registered owner of the car, questioned him about his acquisition and then examined the car in question. Despite a superficial attempt to alter the engine and chassis number it was easily identified as the stolen car.

The owner provided me with details of where he had purchased the car, a small garage just outside Goring on Thames. That would be my next place to visit.

Arriving at the garage I told my colleague I would deal with the man and entered the garage alone. When I introduced myself, he immediately picked up a large spanner, although he did not actually threaten me with it; I was aware he was not going to use it on a nut, at least not a metal nut! It was an aggressive action.

After a few questions to which he could not give me satisfactory answers I told him he was being arrested. He put down the spanner and without any trouble accompanied me to the car. He was transported to Pangbourne police station where the local CID took over the charging procedure.

Shortly afterwards I was approached by an angry detective inspector who told me that the man I had arrested had a conviction for using a firearm whilst resisting arrest and I should not have confronted him on my own. Station instructions stipulate that at least three officers should be present if he was to be interviewed.

Hindsight is all right, but how was I to know about what type of man he was? Thank goodness I am not a confrontational sort of police officer and normally rely on firmness, manners and a degree of common sense.

THE MAN IN THE RED SHIRT

I had spent the day at my Aylesbury office, then in the late afternoon left to return to Oxford. As I was travelling along the A40 and approaching Oxford a call came over the radio that three young men in a dark car were seen leaving the scene of a burglary in Oxford. There was no further description of the car or of the men, other than the driver was wearing a red shirt.

As I was nearing the Headington Roundabout I saw three young men in a car leave the roundabout and start along the A40 towards London. The driver was wearing a red shirt. I called the control room for backup.

I shot round the roundabout to see the suspect car turn right into a side road. I knew this side road split either into a service road in front of a parade of shops, or went behind the shops and came out on the Northern Bypass.

I made a quick decision, went round the roundabout and onto the Northern Bypass and stopped at the entrance to the side road. A few seconds later the car appeared, I drove in front of it forcing it to stop, got out, removed the keys from the ignition of their car and ordered the occupants not to get out. A few minutes later a traffic patrol car arrived and the three men were taken into custody.

On reflection, if those three men had got out and made a run for it, or worse, decided to have a go at me, I would have been in trouble as I had left my short truncheon and handcuffs under the seat of my police car.

A few days later the detective sergeant who was dealing with the burglaries and the arrested men told me he had put my name forward for a commendation for keen observation and quick action in making the arrests.

The next day I was called into the chief superintendent's office. He told me that if my actions had been carried out by a detective constable he would have had no hesitation in endorsing the commendation but as a detective sergeant the action taken by me was what would be expected of an officer of my rank. I did not receive a commendation.

I could not see the reasoning in his logic!

RADIO OXFORD

Just another little story to show how time has changed the police procedures over the years and I believe not for the better.

In the early 1980's I was walking along the Banbury Road in Oxford when I met a man called Chris who I had not seen for at least twenty years. He used to be a racing motorcyclist and it was in this context that we originally met.

We had coffee together in a nearby cafe and discussed careers. He told me he hosted a programme on Radio Oxford and when I mentioned my job with the Stolen Car Squad he invited me there and then into the Radio Oxford studio so that I could be interviewed by him about my work.

In those days the force had a Public Relations Officer and only he or other authorised senior officers were allowed to talk to the press, or go on the radio or television. This procedure was strictly enforced.

Knowing about these restrictions I declined the invitation to speak on the radio but accepted the invitation to look over the studio. Whilst at the studio my friend contacted Force Headquarters and they, surprisingly authorised me to do a short interview there and then on radio about my role in charge of the Car Squad.

In 2012 there was a live report on the local television news programme following a major drug crime bust in Oxford where teams of officers were using battering rams to force their way into several houses.

Interviewed by the television presenter about these raids and outside one of the raided premises was a young female Police Community Support Officer, not even a proper police officer.

Although well-spoken there is no doubt from what she said that she had not been properly briefed and she was making off-the-cuff comments.

In my early days no way would she or any other low rank police officer be allowed to speak to the press. Oh, well I suppose that is progress.

LENNIE THE LION

In the 1980s there was a spate of thefts of farm equipment in the Thames Valley area. Items such as small tractors, stationary engines and the like were being stolen from farms and garden centres.

Following a whisper that they may be sold through an agricultural auction in the grounds of a private zoo at Hoddesdon, Hertfordshire, I decided a visit was worthwhile.

Armed with a shopping list of stolen items Jock and I left early on the morning of the next auction, as we wanted to check out the Lots before the auction started at 10:30am.

We were wading through the hundreds of Lots spread over a couple of acres of the grounds when a man approached and asked if we would give him a hand for a few minutes.

We followed him towards a barn-come cage and as we went round the corner of the barn there was a Land Rover and horse box and in the horse box lay a huge male lion, tranquilised and out sparko.

Apparently, the lion was being transferred from London Zoo to Hoddesdon Private Zoo and on the journey; no doubt unhappy about being so confined it had tried to get out and in doing so had injured itself causing a large cut to its shoulder.

A vet, who had tranquilised the lion, was there with his assistant and was preparing to clean and sew up the injury but there was insufficient room in the horsebox to carry out this operation.

The five of us dragged the lion out of the horsebox, down the ramp and towards the barn door. The other four had his legs and I was pulling his tail.

It was surprising how heavy that lion was and as it was lying down it was wider than the door so we had to part raise it to get it through. Then, just as we had got it through the barn door, I felt its tail twitching, I glanced at Jock who had a worried look in his face, then the lion raised it head and gave a mighty yawn, well, more like a roar; Jock and I ran, fast, very fast and did not stop until we were secure in our police car.

I must admit as I rushed past that lion with his jaws open I was terrified. I had a vivid memory run through my head of a bit of the Stanley Holloway story about when he took his family to a zoo that goes "Our Albert's been swallowed by t' lion."

I did not want a policeman calling at my house and telling my wife, "Your husband's been swallowed by t' lion".

About five minutes later that man was back again asking us to give him a hand. After being assured that the lion had been properly tranquilised Jock and I reluctantly returned to the task of getting the lion fully into the shed and in a position so the vet could carry out his work.

My wife thought I was telling porky pies when I told her I had been lugging about a huge, live male lion.

By the way we did not find any of our stolen agricultural equipment; it was an abortive but exciting day.

OPERATION HGV.

We are quite used to seeing and recognising huge lorries on our roads and some of the names on the sides of these lorries are household names so I was surprised when we had a whiff of information that one of these well-known haulage firms was trading illegally, particularly as they were a large company with a fleet of over 250 lorries.

This firm had depots in Stockport, Lancashire,

Swindon, Wiltshire and Milton Keynes.

Initial enquiries confirmed that these suspicions had some substance so we set up a squad of four officers to look further into this firm's activities. An Incident Room was set up at Faringdon Police Station.

Discreet and extensive enquiries were carried out over several months and it was confirmed that the directors were indeed on the fiddle. In addition to cooking the driver's hours by tampering with the vehicle's tachographs, they were defrauding the taxation authorities of vehicle duty. The tricks they were up to were too numerous to mention here so I will concentrate on just one aspect of this story.

Quite a large number of the vehicles were registered in Southern Ireland, and as it is the way of most police officers they fall shy of dealing with overseas registered vehicles, mainly because they do not understand the paperwork that may be in a foreign language, or know of the different regulations that apply in overseas countries. This company took advantage of this lack of knowledge.

In addition to registering the vehicles overseas there was an element of forgery in the vehicle's documentation and the company records and the company was evading a huge amount of road tax.

After quite a lot of damning information had been

gathered search warrants were obtained and simultaneous raids were made on all three premises. To effect these raids involving three police forces we had to carry out comprehensive briefings to over seventy five police officers.

All the directors were arrested and interviewed by those especially briefed officers who were knowledgeable in this fairly intricate operation. Unfortunately, all the directors were soon lawyered up and refused to answer any questions.

Despite this lack of cooperation the operation was successful and after a very lengthy trial all the directors who were complicit in the firms operations were convicted.

There is always a downside to this type of operation and in particular in this one. As soon as news of the arrests and accusations against the firm became general knowledge, and before the trial began, a lot of their haulage contracts were withdrawn, their business slumped and eventually the whole business collapsed, putting several hundred employees out of work.

There is no doubt that a lot of the workers, particularly the drivers, knew that the firm was trading illegally or evading vehicle tax and I had no sympathy with them but a lot of other innocent workers also lost their jobs.

It was a good and well planned operation and it was estimated that the firm had defrauded the Taxation Authorities of hundreds of thousands of pounds over the five to six years that they had been operating illegally. For instance, back in the 1980's each lorry would have incurred a taxation levy of £1,500 per annum.

THE CHAMPIONS

Whilst on a three month Senior Detective's Course at New Scotland Yard I took up the sport of badminton and after a couple of years attained league standard.

With my partner Tommy we played in the Thames Valley Police Championship and on one occasion won the veterans (over 40 years) runner-up award. Arising from this we were nominated to play in the Number Five Region Badminton Championships of the Police Athletic Association.

At Bedford we played successfully against Hertfordshire Police and then Bedfordshire Police and progressed from there to the semi-final against Hampshire Police.

When we sized up the opposition in the semi-final we

were full of optimism as they were a couple of old duffers, somewhat portly they were both ten to fifteen years older than Tommy and I. We were in for a shock; they totally devastated us with their skill, guile and trickery. Talk about pride before a fall.

Apparently, both the Hampshire players were former county players and played well above our league standard.

ROVER AND ROLEX

Originally reported as a burglary this enquiry was soon directed towards my office when the full story came out.

A couple in their thirties who lived in Watlington, Oxfordshire, reported that during the late evening they had loaded their Rover with holiday luggage in preparation for an early start the next morning as they were going on a three week continental tour.

The man was a helicopter pilot and his wife used to be an airline hostess.

Included in the luggage was the wife's jewellery, including his and hers Rolex watches, both valued at

£5,000 each. The full value of the car and contents was in excess of £20,000.

They claimed the car was properly locked up and they had retired early due to a dawn start but sometime during the night someone, apparently using a neighbour's ladder, had entered through an upstairs back window, taken the car keys off a hook in the hall and had stolen the car and contents.

I was not happy with this claim and neither was an insurance investigator working for the couple's insurance company. The couple were unable to produce receipts for the more expensive items or in relation to the two Rolex watches that the wife claimed she bought in Hong Kong. When I asked her to provide proof that customs duty had been paid on the watches she got into quite a dither.

The Insurance Investigator circulated details of the loss through the loss adjuster's network and a week or so later we had a result. A Loss Adjuster from Truro, Cornwall, had rung up and said he had something to show us.

The Insurance Investigator I was working with was due to go on holiday so I travelled alone to Truro where I met the Loss Adjuster.

He showed me a claim form, made almost two years earlier by a couple, who in preparation for a three week continental tour had loaded their Rover car with luggage the previous night and this included his and hers Rolex watches.

Apparently, on this earlier occasion the thief had borrowed a ladder, entered the back of the house, taken the car keys from a hook in the hall and stole their car and contents.

What a coincidence as the claimants Rover car had the same number as the one I was dealing with and both the husband and wife had the same name as the couple I had earlier interviewed.

At a subsequent interview when I showed the couple the two matching crime files and two matching insurance claims they capitulated and confessed all. Not only were they convicted of attempted deception but also the insurance claim was rejected.

The stupidity of some people is unbelievable.

THE PETROL PILFERER

For the thirty plus years that I have been in the police I can say categorically that the British Police are an upright and honest organisation, the best in the world. However, there are always one or two bad apples.

A constable at Wallingford Police Station was surprised when his early morning task of filling up the police cars with petrol was taken over by his sergeant.

The constable was even more surprised one morning to look through the window and see his sergeant fill up a police car from the pump in the police yard and then a two gallon can that did not go in the police car but into the boot of his private car. The constable passed on his suspicions to a senior officer who called me in to help with the investigation.

Following a meeting with senior officers I went to the Forensic Science Laboratory at Aldermaston and obtained a colourless chemical that I surreptitiously put into the underground petrol tank at Wallingford police station.

Discreet observations were carried out and the sergeant was seen to refuel the police car and then a full petrol can was placed in the boot of his private car.

Later that day and after the sergeant had gone off duty, an inspector and I went to his home address, the sergeant was arrested whilst I siphoned petrol out of the tank of his private car, took it to the Forensic Science Laboratory at Aldermaston where tests showed it contained the chemical I had earlier put in the underground petrol tank at the police station. The sergeant was charged with the theft of petrol.

Due to his local connections, he had been a constable and sergeant at Oxford and Wallingford for over twenty five years; the trial took place at Rugby Crown Court.

He pleaded not guilty and I must admit that when I stood in the witness box and looked at one of my contemporaries in the dock and gave my evidence against him I had mixed feelings. I knew the sergeant quite well, he was almost a mate and I knew my evidence was going to end his career, he was likely to go to prison and it would be devastating to his family.

On the other hand he had brought disgrace to his uniform and the force he represented.

He was found guilty and was sentenced to a period of time in prison.

DVLA AND CHERISHED NUMBERS

The DVLA at Swansea would send to my squad on average two to three enquiries a month relating to cherished numbers, or personalised numbers as some people preferred to call them.

The cherished number enquiries from Swansea nearly always referred to requests for the transfer of numbers supported by false, forged or otherwise dodgy documentation. Some people dreaming of acquiring a number plate with their initials on it, often from old vehicles, will go to extreme lengths and spend a lot of money to fulfil their dreams.

The DVLA were at that time, without a shadow of a doubt very anti-cherished numbers and to this end asked us to carry out rigorous investigations. An awful lot of these applications were turned down and numerous prosecutions ensued.

There were several businesses selling cherished numbers and I agreed with the DVLA policy at that time as some of these firms were sailing close to the wind in their dealings and the forging of documents, particularly MOT certificates and the old log books were rife.

Then there was a sudden change of heart and policy at the DVLA, a change motivated by money. Not only did the DVLA encourage the sale of cherished numbers but started to sell them themselves.

With some of the numbers selling for thousands of pounds, plus there was the transfer fee. All this helped to swell the coffers at the DVLA. Motorists could even dream up their own number and providing it conformed to the recognised format, was not offensive and had not already been allocated, the number would be granted. Money talks.

THE BENTLEY BOYS

Simon Oldroyd was the manager of the Motor Taxation Department of the Bucks County Council and he was good at his job. His work skills improved somewhat when my squad gave him instructions how to detect forged and fraudulent documents. From then on he scrutinised with some zeal vehicle documentation that was brought to his attention by his staff.

About every ten days or so myself or one of my colleagues would visit his office and take away two or three files for further examination and if necessary investigation.

One such file was in relation to the application for the transfer of a cherished number from a pre-war vehicle onto a modern vehicle. There was no doubt the registration number on the old logbook had been altered to make it more appealing, therefore more saleable!

The applicant lived in London so Jock and I went to pay him a visit. He lived in a nice riverside house overlooking the River Thames in Chiswick.

I told Jock that I would not require him to be present at the interview as he had some paperwork to catch up on.

I walked up to the house, knocked on the door and the man who answered was wearing just a shirt or perhaps it was a skirt that barely covered his vitals, then I saw another man come down the stairs behind him similarly attired. At this point I signalled Jock to join me. No way was I going into the house on my own to interview two men so scantily attired.

Interview over we left the house and then saw outside two identical Bentley cars, one bearing the registration mark PEN1S and the other WOM 13, the 13 joined to make it read as a B that equalled WOMB.

Apparently the two men owned a porn shop and a bordello in central London, and it would appear they took their work home.

The application for a transfer of number was refused and he received a police caution for his attempted deception.

SUSIE AND HER BOYFRIEND

It was a warm summer's day when I left the office at Cumnor to go to my bank at Botley, Oxford. I parked in the car park next to a nice looking MGB with the hood down. The car was bearing what was obviously the cherished number of SUS 1 E. As is my wont as I passed this car I looked at the tax disc and could see that it had been crudely altered.

A call to Headquarters Control Room elicited the information that the registration number of SUS 1 E had not been issued. The MGB was on false plates. Now a bit of patience was called for.

About two hours later a young couple laughing and obviously very happy approached and got in the MGB, this is where I intervened. My questions to them did not result in the correct answers so I arrested the couple and took them to St Aldates Police Station where they were placed in the cells whilst I carried out further enquiries. They were no longer a happy laughing couple.

Incidentally, the girl's first name was Susie.

After I had firmly established that the car was in fact stolen from Leeds and on false plates, the couple were charged and bailed to Leeds Magistrates Court.

The young man was a failed student whose parents were Headmaster and Headmistress respectively of two fairly famous private schools in the Leeds area, this may have some connection with why their son had gone off the rails.

When the detective inspector of our Scenes of Crime Department, who was also in charge of the Car Squad for administrative purposes, told me I had to go to and deliver the court papers personally to the Leeds Police and then by appointment see the lad's parents I realised that some intense pressure was being exerted by the parents to get the charges against the young man dropped.

After conferring with the Leeds Police who agreed that no deal would be made, I saw the parents and of course they tried to get the charges dropped, but no way was that going to happen.

The lad and his girl were duly convicted.

A PAKISTANI POSER

Whilst on the topic of cherished numbers, I must impart this little bit of information.

Today if a person used the word Paki when referring to a person from Pakistan this would be considered derogatory and racist. In the 1980's the Pakistani High Commissioner to London had a Jaguar car that bore the cherished number PAK 1.

I wonder if this number has since been changed.

THE WAYS AND MEANS ACT

No you will not find this act in any law book but this made up bit of law is often used by police to deal with criminals who persistently evade the law and who, for their crimes, should receive some form of punishment.

My colleague Jock and I had been on the fringe of a couple of enquiries into a fraud committed by a criminal called Gealing who lived at Leighton Buzzard in Bedfordshire.

I was aware of his reputation of defrauding people out of money through the sale of motor vehicles but had not actually met him.

He was engaged in the import from Holland of clapped out, high mileage Dutch ex-GPO Volkswagen vans. At his little garage in Leighton Buzzard he cut holes in the side panels and inserted plain glass windows, then fitted a rough wooden platform on which he put a second-hand mattress, fitted a small metal sink with no taps, and the waste water just ran down the outside of the van, then he constructed a sort of worktop that was fitted beside the sink, and then the 'kitchen' was completed with the fitting of a Calor gas ring and bottle.

I must say Gealing was a very good paint sprayer and he resprayed these old vehicles to a high standard with a coat of bright blue paint. Superficially they looked almost like new from a distance. He was converting beat up old wrecked vehicles into campervans.

The vehicles were then registered with the DVLA, and as their date of manufacture was undetermined, they were given a "Q" plate with the date of registration being the year the conversion was carried out.

Gealing then advertised the vehicles for sale in Australia, New Zealand and South African holiday brochures and magazines, complete with a glowing description and photographs.

At that time, the mid 1980's, a large number of youngsters were coming over from those countries for a holiday or on a gap year break and a campervan was an ideal mode of transport for them, and there was a good market for this type of vehicle. Gealing would ask for the money up front for the vehicle.

It was not illegal to sell these vans but the buyers were paying a high price for a pile of rubbish and there was an element of deception by the seller.

On arrival in this country the tourists would ring Gealing and he would arrange to meet them in a café in a street in north London. There he would hand over the registration document and keys then point to the shiny newly registered vehicle a hundred yards away, and then as the new owner went to the vehicle Gealing would scarper before the new buyer may have realised they had been conned.

After speaking to my contact at the Customs Office at Felixstowe, a couple of months later we received information from them that Gealing was importing twelve Volkswagen vans from Holland. He was expanding his business.

The customs officer told me the vans were due to arrive in England on a certain day so on that day my colleague and I went to Felixstowe Docks where we located the twelve vehicles.

We found Gealing asleep on a bail of cloth on the dockside whilst he waited for twelve students from Cambridge to arrive whom he had paid £25 each to drive them to his property in Leighton Buzzard.

We woke him up, introduced ourselves and told him that we intended to examine all the vehicles. He then got irate, became very rude and obstructive and would not hand over the keys for the vehicles. Truth be known we may not have had the authority to examine them as they were on private property.

We had not travelled all that way for nothing so I spoke to my friend the Customs Officer and that did the trick.

The Customs Officer told Gealing that they were going to examine all the vehicles for drugs and then Gealing had to hand over the keys. A team of customs officers promptly took off all four wheels of the twelve vans and then removed the inner tubes, deflated them so that they could feel for suspected drugs. No drugs were found.

Gealing was really enraged as he expected the custom officers to put right the tyres that had been removed but they were not obliged to do so.

Gealing had to arrange for a local tyre company to refit all the tyres and wheels, all 48 of them. He was furious, particularly as his drivers had by then arrived and were not happy with the delay.

We were not finished with Mr Gealing. It was pretty obvious that the students would not be insured, may not be licensed and none of the vans were taxed so we rang the Suffolk Police Traffic Department and put them in the picture.

As the drivers left Felixstowe in convoy there was a police reception party waiting for them. Gealing, as the owner of the vans was charged and convicted for numerous offences in permitting the use of the vehicles without the necessary documentation.

This brought to an end Gealing's import business.

I did meet Gealing on one other occasion. This was about six months later at Leighton Buzzard Car Auctions. As soon as he saw me he made a very quick exit.

A WATERY WALLY

The terms of reference for the Car Squad were fairly loose and we would investigate any crime relating to any mode of transport, including boats.

Boats have engines and come under our terms of reference and over the years quite a lot of boat thefts and related crimes came our way.

There was this man called Walter who lived in a village near Maidenhead and after his boat sunk in the River Thames he made an insurance claim for its loss. The Loss Adjuster, an ex-police officer, working for his insurance company contacted me, as he was not happy with the claim. He had good reason to be unhappy.

I interviewed Walter at his home; well it was more like a hovel, dark, dingy and smelly, as was the man. He was a single man aged about fifty years and rather corpulent, he was also a heavy smoker.

Walter told me he took his motor powered boat out to a quiet backwater on the River Thames to do a bit of fishing then on the way back to the moorings his boat hit a submerged object, the boat was holed and it sunk about fifty yards from the bank.

He said he swam to the bank, walked about a quarter of a mile to the nearest unmade road, then went to a pub to have a whisky or two to relieve his shock and steady his nerves. He then went home to get changed.

After taking a statement from Walter I told him to come with me and show me where the boat went down. I took him in the police car to the nearest spot to where he said his boat went down.

We then walked the quarter of a mile across rough ground to the riverbank. I took the opportunity to observe him, and even walking that short distance he was out of breath and decidedly unhealthy looking, I very much doubted that he could swim even fifty feet.

As we got back to the car he was about to get in the car but I said, "No." I then told Walter we would walk to the pub he said he'd visited. This was about a mile from where I had parked the car and in the opposite direction and by the time we reached it Walter was just about all in.

Before we entered I pointed out to him that someone in the pub would remember a man, soaking wet from swimming in the river and buying a drink, probably with soggy notes. Walter realised I had not fallen for his story and then admitted that he had made up the tale about the visit to the pub. The first lie had been revealed.

I took him back to his hovel, then I went to the nearest store, bought an air freshener and fumigated the passenger seat of the police car but despite this I am convinced that the nasty smell of Walter followed me about for the next few days.

I contacted the River Authority and they confirmed they had no record of a submerged object or of the claimant's sunken boat in the area indicated by Walter.

I then went to the marina where Walter moored his boat and when I mentioned the loss of the boat to the owner of the marina he said that Walter's boat had sunk once before at its moorings and when later lifted the reason became clear, the boat was in a very bad state, a bit like Walter, and several planks had sprung leaks letting in water.

We went to the mooring in question and there we could just see in the somewhat murky water that Walter's boat had in fact sunk for the second time at its moorings. Walter had made a false insurance claim.

At my second visit to Walter's abode I told him that he had lied on his insurance claim and to me, and he would not be paid out for the loss of the boat and he may be prosecuted for attempted deception.

At the end of the day the insurance company concerned did not pay out and were reluctant to support a prosecution so Walter was cautioned and that is where it ended.

Walter did incur a monetary penalty in that the owner of the marina raised then disposed of the boat, and Walter had to pay the bill so he did not get off entirely scot-free.

THE SEAT OF THE FIRE

At 4:30am one morning a lorry driver leaving his depot near Witney noticed smoke coming from a manufacturing unit on a small industrial estate so he called the Fire Brigade.

Before the fire was extinguished a furniture factory and a plastic factory next door were burned to the ground. As the cause of the fire had not been determined I, as a so-called arson expert, was called in to help the furniture factory's insurance company with the enquiries.

I applied for a copy of the fire brigade report and this showed that the cause of the fire was given as spontaneous combustion in a pile of sawdust in the furniture factory. I was not happy with this explanation.

I know that the fire brigade are usually busy and unless an expert in arson is called in the officer in charge of the tender will make a rough guess as to the cause of the fire. Spontaneous combustion can occur in hay and straw ricks but I very much doubt if a small pile of dry sawdust could so ignite. Sawdust is an inert material so more enquiries were called for.

The furniture factory employed about eight workers but they were now out of work as were the workers at the plastic factory.

After interviewing the furniture factory boss and his staff and carrying out further enquiries I had not progressed very far. The factory was fairly modern, as was their electrical equipment and it was not thought an electrical fault could have caused the fire.

There was no suspicion of arson. All health and safety regulations had been complied with.

I decided to interview the lorry driver who reported the fire to the fire brigade. He told me that as he drove past the premises he saw smoke coming out of the doors and through the roof. He got out of his cab, prised open the sliding doors and through the gap he could just see that the fork lift truck parked alongside the charging point was well alight and the fire had by then reached the factory roof.

This did not make sense as the furniture factory had

an up-and-over door and they did not have a fork lift truck. I then realised the driver was talking about the plastic factory next door and this is where the fire had started. The driver confirmed that at that time the furniture factory was not alight.

The driver had to travel to the nearest telephone box in Witney to call out the fire brigade. (No mobile phones in those days,) and by the time the fire brigade arrived both places were pretty well gutted.

Later I located a man who worked at another factory and he told me something interesting. As he left work at 4:30pm each day, he got in his car and switched on his radio. As he drove past the plastic factory if his radio crackled he looked across and saw through the open door that the forklift truck was alongside the charging point. If his radio did not crackle then he saw that the forklift truck was being used outside the premises.

There is no doubt that the evidence of these two persons suggested the cause of the fire was an electrical fault in the fork lift truck charging point in the plastic factory, and the fire had not started in the furniture factory.

An interesting side issue; the furniture factory boss had submitted a claim to his insurer, General Accident for the loss of the premises and consequential losses, and the plastic factory owner claimed against the furniture factory insurers as well.

The Legal and General Insurance Company, the plastic factory's insurers, had to foot the bill for the loss of both premises.

OBSERVATIONS ON THE VILLAGE LADY

"As a result of information received"," how many times have I heard that expression? Well the information I received was of a couple that lived in a village near Watlington who were in possession of a stolen vehicle?

The information did not come from a good source and was vague so I was a bit sceptical at first. I wanted to see the car being used so I could carry out a document check into its history.

The trouble I encountered was that when not in use it would appear the suspect car was garaged. The husband had a company car that was usually parked on the driveway outside the house. It was a low key enquiry so when in the area I did a bit of observation, particularly when the lady's children went to or from school, just in case she took the car out of the garage at these times.

The couple lived at the end of a close so it was difficult to maintain observation. I usually parked my car at the top end of the close and in a position to see if the car was taken out of its garage.

After I had maintained observation half a dozen times I was considering making a more direct approach when there was a knock on the car's window. An angry man said that he had seen me parked in the same spot on several occasions and he had been watching me, he wanted to know what I was up to.

Some sort of explanation was necessary and I had one ready. I told him that I worked for the Milk Marketing Board and I had a long standing arrangement to be at this particular spot at certain times of the day on the off chance I could meet up with my boss and hand over the record of milk yields obtained from the local farms. I do not like telling untruths but some explanation was necessary to allay his worries. He was reasonably happy with this explanation.

I was in the same position a couple of weeks later when there was a knock on the car window, it was that man again. This time he appeared somewhat apologetic. He said that he was going through a rather messy divorce and his wife had instructed a private investigator to spy on him and he originally thought I was that PI. After assurances I was not a private investigator I accepted his apology and he went away happy.

Shortly after the man walked away I had a sort of result, a delivery van called at the suspect's house, the wife came out and opened the garage door I drove down the close, turned round and then could see in the garage there was no car there and from the amount of clutter in the garage a car had not been in the garage for a very long time.

I concluded we had been fed some false information and had wasted a lot of time. That's all part of police work.

THE HIDDEN JAGUAR.

It was a murky day, not the right ambience to be out and about, when we had a telephone call from a farmer who informed us that a man who owned a smallholding adjacent to his farm on the Oxfordshire/Wiltshire border had a suspect stolen Jaguar on his (the smallholder's) premises so we had to leave our warm office and do a bit of leg work.

By coincidence, we had earlier commenced enquiries into the reported theft of two Jaguars from the Faringdon area and the smallholder's name had come up but we had not yet taken any further steps into this aspect of the enquiry.

Dave, one of my lads from the Oxford Squad, and I went to the smallholding. The suspect man was not there so in his absence, and I admit, without a search warrant we casually searched the outbuildings and surrounding area but could not find any trace of the Jaguar.

We returned to our office at Cumnor and shortly after I received another call from the farmer. He told me that he knew we had not found the car! How did he know? He must have been watching us through a pair of binoculars. We confirmed our lack of success. He then said it was still there and added,

"Go back and look in the woodpile."

We went back but on our second visit the smallholder was there. After introducing ourselves we told him the purpose of our visit and after a cursory search of the outbuildings, just for effect, we went to a woodpile that consisted of pine logs stacked on end and about eight feet high, it looked like a big wigwam.

After pulling half a dozen logs away we found a stolen Jaguar concealed inside.

The car was seized, the man arrested and later convicted of the theft of the two Jaguars.

I have often wondered why the farmer did not tell us on the first instance to check inside the woodpile, perhaps he wanted to watch and check on our efficiency in conducting a search.

On the other hand the thief must have thought that we had made a pretty thorough search.

DIGGING DEEP FOR TREASURE

Another case involving a concealed vehicle shows how far criminals will go to hide the spoils of their crime. This case, following some good information meant we obtained a warrant to search a plant contractor's site near Bracknell, Berkshire, where we believed there was a stolen JCB digger. There were a couple of other diggers on site but not the one we were looking for.

We were about to give up the search when on of my men from the Bracknell Squad noticed a large area of disturbed soil. After some deliberation we decided to investigate further. Using one of the other JCB's we dug out the area of disturbed soil to find the stolen JCB buried in a huge hole and covered by tarpaulins. It must have been eight feet down.

We wondered how long it would have remained so interred before it was resurrected and put into circulation!

A successful case against the plant contractor was eventually concluded.

WATCH YOUR LANGUAGE!

The preceding story reminds me of yet another incident that involved a colleague who was dealing with the theft of a JCB digger.

There was this belligerent Irish plant owner, well known for his short temper that owned a yard just outside Witney, Oxfordshire. Early one morning he went to his yard to find it had been broken into and a nearly new JCB digger stolen.

He was somewhat irate as one of his workers was scheduled that morning to carry out a very important and lucrative job. No digger and an idle worker were not to his liking, as he would lose a lot of money on the contract. He telephoned Witney Police Station and reported the theft of his £35,000 digger.

About 45 minutes later a busy and harassed

probationer police officer turned up to take a crime report and carry out the usual enquiries. He was confronted by a tirade of abuse from the owner over the delay in responding to the call and the officer responded by giving the JCB owner a few sharp words of his own.

A sequel to this little spat was that the plant owner made an official complaint about the police officer's abusive attitude.

A superintendent and a sergeant from the Complaints and Discipline Department of the Thames Valley Police went to see the plant owner. They took statements from him, his driver and other witnesses to the argument; quite a bulky file was compiled against the officer.

By responding with like for like language to the abusive plant owner, the probationer was subject of an in-depth enquiry and interviewed by a superintendent and his sergeant, that involved statement taking and a comprehensive report being sent to the Police Complaints Bureau.

Several months later a hearing was held in which the constable had a legal representative supplied by the Police Federation. It was considered the constable had been abusive and he received a severe caution.

Surely there is a total imbalance in that a £35,000

crime receives little attention, just the submission of a crime report by a probationer constable and an entry on the Police National Computer, but a few inappropriate words by this police officer required such a vigorous and time consuming investigation conducted by a superintendent and his sergeant?

MOLES

I was in Chipping Norton Police Station having a cup of tea with a couple of coppers when the conversation got round to the unusual items that had been reported stolen. One of the constables said that a couple of weeks earlier he had received a report of the theft of three moles. No, not those furry little things that live underground but mechanical moles.

The officer told me no arrests had been made and the stolen items had not been recovered so I decided to check the crime file to see if further enquiries were warranted.

The three moles had been stolen from a construction site near Chipping Norton, and as I suspected no enquiries had been carried out but a file had been created and then filed.

During this period of time, I understand it still is the procedure today, on each working day all the crime files were assessed by the CID Office Manager, usually a civilian, whose job it was to determine the possibility of the property being recovered or an arrest made. If there were no obvious leads the crime was immediately screened out and the papers filed, in other words, binned.   This is what happened in relation to the crime report on the stolen moles.

I picked up the file to see if I could find if there were any lines of enquiry that I could follow up, after all the total value of the three moles was in excess of £30,000 and I believed further enquiries were justified.

Back at my office I telephoned the West Midlands company employee who had reported the loss of the machines and he informed me that the three electronically controlled machines had not been recovered; also that one of them had been malfunctioning at the time of the theft.   I obtained from him the machines serial numbers and the name of the manufacturer/supplier. (The police at Chipping Norton had not asked for this information so it is not surprising there was little chance of recovery.)

My second call was to the manufacturer/supplier and the manager there told me that the moles were made in Germany and his company was the sole supplier of the moles in the United Kingdom, the only supplier of spare parts and had the mechanical knowledge to service or repair them. I left the serial number of the three stolen moles with him with a request to contact me if any of them came to his attention.

About two weeks later this manager did call me to say that one of the moles, the defective one, had been brought to their premises for repair. He provided me with the name and address of the man who had brought in the mole, now a suspect. He lived in Hampshire.

One of my contemporaries, John Smallbone was then a detective constable with the Hampshire Constabulary Stolen Vehicle Squad, and he was good and reliable so I was happy for him to take over the enquiry.

The next day John telephoned me to say that with a search warrant he and his colleague had visited the suspect's premises and recovered the other two stolen moles. The suspect was arrested and handed over to the Chipping Norton police as the original crime came within their jurisdiction.

The case was solved. £30,000 worth of property recovered and the thief ultimately arrested and convicted. Just three telephone calls that only took me a few minutes and the crime file was successfully brought to a satisfactory conclusion and closed. So much for the policy of screening out crime files.

CONTAINERS AND ASIANS

My squad had been investigating the theft and exportation of high value vehicles and this lead us to look closely at three Asians. I cannot recall what country they originally came from but they were permanent residents in England. All we had to do was catch them in the act.

To help us we were liaising with the Belgian police via a friend and colleague Detective Inspector Ronnie Van Den Hoeck who was in charge of their Stolen Vehicle Squad based in Antwerp.

At our request a watch was kept on Felixstowe Docks, as this was where the stolen cars were being exported from in containers. Subsequently we had a call from the Customs office that these Asians had a container delivered to the docks and it was shortly to be shipped to Antwerp. Now was the time for action.

With a couple of my lads I went to Felixstowe and at our request the Customs Officer broke the seal on the container and inside were two top of the range Mercedes cars worth about £150,000. Leaning against the outermost car was a large sign

'Allah is Great'.

No doubt this was a friendly message from the English Asians to the Belgian Asians.

After establishing the cars were indeed stolen the container was re-sealed. We had the three Asians in England on ice but firstly we wanted to catch the receivers in Antwerp. In due course the container was loaded on a ship and sent on its way to Belgium.

On arrival at Antwerp the container was picked up by the Belgian Asians and taken to a remote farmhouse, discreetly followed by the Belgian police under the supervision of Detective Inspector Ronnie Van Den Hoeck.

When the Asians broke the seal and opened the container they were confronted by that friendly message from their English colleagues amended slightly, it now read

'Allah is Great, but the British Car Squad are Greater'.

As they were pondering this message the Belgian police swooped and all the suspects both sides of the North Sea were arrested, eventually convicted and hundreds of thousands of pounds worth of stolen cars recovered.

THE HUNGERFORD HOWLER

A young police constable stationed at Hungerford gave me a call after he had received a report of a stolen vehicle. The circumstances just did not add up.

The brief story was that an 18 year old lad called Colin, whose father had given him a sporty Ford Escort RS for his birthday, had driven the car to his local pub, so local that it was less than 50 yards from where he lived.

The lad had a couple of pints and then went outside to find his car had been stolen from the pub car park. He telephoned the local police and reported its theft.

Later that evening his car was found crashed about two miles from the pub. Apparently on a sharp corner it had been driven through a hedge and a tree stump had ripped out the underside. It was a total write-off.

When interviewed by a local police officer, Colin said that he made the call to the police from the Public House. The constable who had visited the scene enquired of the Landlord and confirmed that Colin had not phoned the police from the pub. The officer checked the car park to see if the thief left any debris such as glass at the scene when the car was broken into. No such debris was found.

I received a request for help from the young constable and when he and I interviewed Colin for the second time, his father accompanied him. The lad said he was so distressed by the theft of his newly acquired car that he meant to say he had walked home and rang the police from there and not from the pub. This was his first mistake or perhaps the first lie.

What the lad did not know was that we already had a record that the call had been made from a public telephone box situated midway between the pub and where the car had been crashed. Confronted with this new information the lad then said that he must have been so dazed by the theft he could have possibly walked around for a bit.

He would have walked in a daze a mile to the phone box in the same direction the car had been driven. I think not.

His father was a forceful character, the boss of a large business with a fleet of cars and vans. He constantly interrupted the questioning and tried unsuccessfully to dominate the interview.

The lad was arrested and charged but for some inexplicable reason the Crown Prosecution Service decided not to prosecute. I often wonder if the father had exerted some influence to bring about this decision. I was not happy about this outcome in fact I was decidedly unhappy.

I made enquiries of the insurance company who would have to deal with the claim for the damaged vehicle and they also were unhappy with the outcome of the accident and police action.

The father, who insured his fleet of vehicles with the same company, had been making waves, big waves and demanded early payment but the insurance company had by then appointed an insurance investigator to look into this matter.

The investigator gave me a little bit of information about Colin so I went to the newspaper library at Newbury looked up a report in the local paper printed some eighteen months earlier about this lad and what a gem of information it was.

Apparently Colin had gone into a local fish and chip shop face covered and wielding a baseball bat. He demanded the contents of the till. The owner said,

"Don't be daft Colin, what would your dad say if he knew what you are up to."

Colin fled.

He was arrested, charged and convicted of attempted armed robbery. A conviction he had failed to declare when he took out insurance on the Escort.

The alleged theft of the car was scrubbed off the police records and the insurance company refused to pay out on the claim based on this non-disclosure of a serious conviction. At least I got some sort of satisfactory result.

CEDRIC THE CHAUFFEUR

Dave and I had been on enquiries in the south of the Thames Valley area and were on our way back to our office at Oxford. Just after passing through the village of Nettlebed we saw a clump of soil in the roadway and signs that a vehicle had hit the verge. A bit further on there was another clump of soil. Continuing, we came across a Morris Minor travelling about 20mph and weaving about. It did not take much working out that the driver was drunk.

Pulling in front of the Minor we forced it to stop. The driver got out, well no, to be more accurate, he staggered out of the car confirming our original thoughts and he stank of alcohol.

Dave called up for a uniformed officer with a breathalyser kit to attend. Meanwhile I noted that the front left tyre was punctured, no doubt caused by hitting the verge.

The driver, a little man, aged about sixty years put up his fists said he was a boxing champion when he was in the army and offered to fight us. We ignored his gesturing, as he was no real threat.

I then pointed out to him that he had a flat front tyre he went to the back of the car got out the jack and instead of putting it under the car he put it under the hub cap of the front wheel. As he started to turn the handle, as expected the hubcap popped off and hit him he tumbled backward – into a six foot ditch. Lucky for him it was quite a gradual slope and there was no water in the bottom.

With much mirth at his predicament we helped him back up the bank.

He then got the tyre wrench out of the boot and tried to undo the wheel nuts by turning it the wrong way. We did not let on that he was doing it all wrong.

Another call was made to Headquarters and we learnt that there were no police cars in the vicinity that could come to our assistance.

Although the Act of Parliament that introduced the breathalyser was in force the old act had not been repealed so I arrested the driver under the old act and took him to Wallingford Police Station where he was breathalysed – he was well over the limit. He was duly charged and convicted.

Thank goodness we were on that stretch of road at that time and were able to stop this man as further enquiries showed that he was a chauffeur for a wealthy family who lived near Nettlebed and he was on his way in the family runabout to pick up two children from a private school at Wallingford.

He was so inebriated that those children would have been in grave danger on their way home.

Cedric was dismissed from his employ so he suffered twofold for his drunken driving.

RISBOROUGH RALLY CARS

During the 1960/1970s I was a keen rally driver and I also followed the activities of other rally drivers so I knew about Danny Longwick. He lived in the town of Princes Risborough in Buckinghamshire and his wealthy dad had either given him the money or sponsored his Ford Escort rally car.

Danny Longwick's name often appeared in the weekly 'Motoring News' as he was a reasonably successful driver. He was also a bullish driver and quite often his car a Ford Escort RS would suffer damage both mechanical and bodily.

I am a great one for looking at patterns of car thefts and recoveries and at first I was mystified why stolen cars mainly Ford Escorts were being abandoned in the Princes Risborough area with bits missing.

Danny's rally exploits and these abandoned cars eventually gelled together to form a pattern. My colleagues and I strongly suspected he was the car thief so closer attention was paid to his exploits and to his father's business premises where he garaged his rally car.

Later Danny expanded his illegal acts by stripping the nicked cars and selling the stolen parts via the 'Exchange and Mart' magazine.

When we raided his premises he was caught in the act of transferring bits from a stolen car onto his rally car, he did not have a leg to stand on and under caution admitted everything.

That was the end of his rally career as his licence to rally was withdrawn. He also received a short prison sentence.

CAR SERVICES ON THE CHEAP

In connection to this previous story, Danny Longwick had a couple of hangers-on who were motor mechanics and I have no doubt helped Danny with his car stripping but we did not have sufficient evidence to charge them. In fact they turned into informants.

These two mechanics worked for a small garage near Princes Risborough. The owner ran the filling station and the mechanics carried out car servicing and minor repairs on his behalf in the garage behind.

Their little scam was simple and virtually detection proof but our informants were good. When a car came in for a service they would drain the oil from the engine and gearbox, filter it through muslin or some other cloth to remove any impurities and then put the oil back into the engine and gearbox. Likewise with the oil filters these would be removed cleaned with paraffin and replaced. Spark plugs would be sandblasted reset and reinstated. Other parts that required changing during the service were wherever possible the refurbished ones.

The owner of the car would be invoiced the full amount for all the new oils and parts. Meanwhile the new parts that should have been fitted to the car during the service were taken away and used by the two mechanics as they were also moonlighting at car servicing.

Obviously in their moonlighting operation they had no need to buy oil and parts but the owners were charged the full price for the stolen items. It was a neat little scam profitable and virtually foolproof.

The garage owner was aghast when we told him how the scheme worked and he was mightily relieved when they were convicted at court.

GREEN SHIELD STAMPS

As time went by, we as a squad became experts in identifying stolen vehicles no matter how well the thief may have disguised them. But one car, a Lotus Cortina gave us a real headache. We knew it was stolen but what was its true identity?

The thief owned a Lotus Cortina that he had crashed and in doing so had comprehensively destroyed the bodywork but the mechanics were reasonably good. So he stole a standard Ford Cortina and transferred practically all the parts from his Lotus Cortina car onto the stolen car including its identifying features and number plates.

He made a really good job of it. He had converted the stolen standard Ford Cortina into a Lotus Cortina complete with badges, colour scheme and all the other goodies and the stolen car originally worth £1,500 was now worth at least £6,000.

Despite an in depth examination and a search of literally thousands of stolen Ford records we just could not match up a Lotus Cortina to any stolen basic Ford Cortina.

Eventually, by a system of elimination we concluded that it would appear to have been a Ford Cortina stolen from a married couple that lived in High Wycombe.

We took it to their house where the man examined it fairly closely and declared it was not his car and then his wife said,

"I can tell if it was our car. When we were courting we had a blazing row, my then boyfriend pulled into a filling station filled up and when he got back in the car; I snatched the Green Shield stamps out of his hand, licked them and stuck them on the floor under the carpet on the passenger side."

She went to the car lifted the carpet and there were the Green Shield stamps. That spurred the husband to make a closer examination and he found several other minor points that confirmed it was in fact the car stolen from him about a year earlier. We had enough evidence to arrest and charge the thief.

The case came up at High Wycombe Magistrates Court where the thief pleaded not guilty but that pile of Green Shield stamps proved the point in favour of the prosecution case and he was convicted.

This was not the end of the matter as the thief later made claim to the car and this came up at another sitting of the magistrates under the Police Property Act.

His claim was that the parts transferred from his Lotus Cortina onto the stolen vehicle were by far a lot more valuable than the standard Cortina he had stolen. He had a good and valid point but the magistrates ruled that a thief should not benefit from his crime and his claim to the car was refused.

The owner of the stolen Cortina was very pleased with his upgraded car, which was now a valuable Lotus Cortina.

CHRIS - THE LIABILITY

For my sins I was given a detective constable at the Bracknell office that was a right mixture of good and stupid. I shall call him Chris. He had encyclopaedic knowledge of commercial vehicles, was an excellent thief taker and came with some excellent informants. He was reasonably good with paperwork and a first class interrogator. He could encourage even the most hardened criminal to open up his heart and admit all his crime.

Another trait he had was the luck of the devil. If he decided to stop a car for a routine check it would be loaded with drugs or be stolen.

On the other side he was totally unreliable and in some ways very childish. On one occasion he was after a tasty bit of information from an informant and to get him to come across with this information, without consent from a senior officer he took some cannabis from the police crime property store and passed it on to the informant for his personal use.

The information was good and a couple of useful arrests were made and stolen property recovered however an internal audit showed the discrepancy in the crime property.

This is always a serious matter as firstly the drugs were required as a court exhibit and secondly it cast a shadow over every police officer that had access to the store.

Shortly after hearing about the internal audit Chris asked confidentially to speak to me and he then admitted he had taken the drugs.

I told him that I had no option but to report the matter to a senior officer and he would probably face a court case and dismissal from the police.

As I mentioned, he had the luck of the devil. The chief superintendent who was given the task of investigating the 'theft of drugs' was his close personal friend and Chris used to service his car.

Chris admitted he had taken the drugs but came up with the story that after he had given a bit of training to a probationer officer about drugs, he was going to replace the drugs back in the store but he had lost them. It was a cover-up and he evaded prosecution.

On another occasion I went to Bracknell police station and again Chris asked to speak to me confidentially. He then said,

"I have done something stupid,"

Anticipating the worst I asked him what? He then said that some weeks earlier he had married a girl he did not like, in fact he detested her. I thought he was referring to his long-time girlfriend that he was living with. Apparently not, it was someone he had met more recently and they had obtained a Special Licence to get married.

To compound the matter further he used to live in his own house with his girlfriend and was in receipt of a police rent allowance for that property and after his marriage he let the old girlfriend remain in the house. Meanwhile he obtained rented accommodation elsewhere for himself and his new wife.

Following my questioning he acknowledged that he was obtaining a rent allowance from the police for the house he owned and a housing allowance for the property he lived in with his new wife. Again he could have faced prosecution for obtaining benefit by deception.

I ordered him to immediately inform the housing officer at Police Headquarters, Kidlington, and offer to repay back the full amount he had fraudulently obtained. Once again he got out of the situation without any charge or disciplinary action.

On yet another occasion I went to the Bracknell office and he was missing. I later learnt that the previous evening, laden with a few alcoholic drinks he tried to climb a flagpole fell to the ground and broke his ankle, which meant he was off duty for a couple of weeks. Meanwhile I had all the extra work to clear up his files.

The final straw came a few months after this episode. We were dealing with the theft of a couple of Aston Martin cars from Reading and as we knew the name of the suspect an arrest warrant was obtained.

Whilst at home late one evening I received a telephone call from Greenford Police in London that the suspect had been arrested driving a stolen Vauxhall Astra. The police agreed to hold him overnight.

I rang Chris and told him the good news. I said that I would pick him up at 7am the next morning and we would go together to Greenford and interview the suspect and transfer him to Reading Police Station.

As arranged, at 7am I arrived at Chris' house, knocked on the door and after some time his girlfriend answered. She told me that Chris had left alone, contrary to my instructions, at 6am for Greenford. I was furious.

I went to Greenford and found Chris had already interviewed the suspect. In a professional way we dealt with the necessary paperwork and then took the prisoner to Reading Police Station where he was duly charged.

As I had left my police car at Greenford Police

Station we had to go all the way back to London to pick it up. This was an entirely unnecessary journey. I had had enough of his wayward actions.

I arranged to see Chris at his house the next morning, I told him that I had given him too many chances and for deliberately ignoring my orders he was off the squad as from that time.

He went back to general CID duties at Slough. I do not believe he was all bad just hyperactive and he did not think out the consequences of his sometimes daft actions.

That was not the last I saw of Chris as after I had been retired from the police for a couple of years I saw him in Reading with a low loader lorry carrying a JCB digger.

He had apparently been kicked out of the police, not that it would have worried him too much, as I later found out that when he was in the police and even whilst on my squad he owned two lorries and employed two drivers and had a lucrative haulage contract business. The force in my opinion was well rid of him.

THE PRICELESS ROVER

As anyone with knowledge of the motor trade will tell you there are no real bargains when buying a motor vehicle, a real snip is a myth and if a car is too cheap then there is almost certainly something wrong with it. But in one incident I dealt with a buyer who really did get a bargain, a fantastic bargain.

There was a man who lived with his wife in a small village on the outskirts of Abingdon. He was the owner of a beautiful 1950s Rover 90 car, a classic worth between £5,000 and £6,000.

This car was the love of his life and he cherished it dearly. This beautiful car only came out of its garage on a few occasions for a polish and when he occasionally took it to the Rover Club rallies.

He also loved his equally beautiful girlfriend. But when his wife found out about the second of his loves sparks began to fly.

His wife literally kicked him out of the family home. He slunk away with his girlfriend, leaving his family and the Rover locked away in the garage, not the family locked away, just the Rover! He finally set up home with his girlfriend in Scotland.

He lost his job and the company car that went with it so he was soon in financial trouble.

A few months later finding himself almost out of funds he wrote to his wife asking her to sell his Rover and send him the money. She knew what the car was worth but now was payback time. As a dutiful wife she complied with his request, put the cars details on a postcard and placed it in the window of the local newsagents. It was soon sold for the advertised price - £50.

Needless to say he was infuriated to receive in the post the fifty pounds for his five thousand pound plus car, so he contacted Abingdon Police Station and reported that his wife had stolen the car and then he made an insurance claim for its loss.

The theft report filtered down to my office so I went to see the man's wife as she was the nearest. She told me the full sorry story and showed me the letter received from her husband. Yes, he had asked her to sell his Rover but he had not stipulated what price she should sell it for.

He may have valued the car at over £5,000 but to her it was a rival and she was glad to see the back of it.

As far as I was concerned there was no theft, no crime and the man had no recourse to an insurance claim. That's the penalty of running a wife and a mistress.

There is a motorist out there who is driving around in a beautiful classic Rover car worth about £5,000 that he bought for £50. That's what the famous antique dealer David Dickenson would have called 'the real deal'.

GREY IMPORTS

In the 1980s there was a big problem with what was then called 'grey imports'. These cars were imported into the United Kingdom, which did not meet the required Construction and Use standards. In other words they were made overseas to a standard lower than that required in this country.

The problem was the same in the United States. That country was one of the first to require the fitting of catalytic converters to vehicles and their 'grey import' problems were cars not fitted with these cat converters. It was soon a big headache over there.

My friend Gene, who was in the California Highway Patrol, had one such problematic vehicle that required looking into. It was a Mercedes exported from the United Kingdom into the USA via the San Diego docks. It did not have a catalytic converter so the importer's request for registration by the DMV (Department of Motor Vehicles) was turned down.

How odd that a few weeks later after it had been insured it was found burnt out up in the boondocks and an insurance claim sent to the insurance company.

Gene was convinced the importer had set his own car alight but was having difficulty in proving it. This is where I came in.

When the attempt to register the Mercedes with the DMV failed the importer produced a purchase invoice showing he had bought the car for £14,500 from a dealership in London. Gene sent me a photocopy of the purchase invoice and asked me to check it out.

My trip to London was worthwhile as the dealership's copy of the purchase invoice showed that the importer had indeed purchased the Mercedes from them, for £4,500, not £14,500. The importer had obviously forged the invoice by putting a 1 in front of the 4.

Armed with a copy of the original invoice that I sent him, Gene arrested the man and charged him with attempted deception on the insurance company. He was duly convicted and obviously his claim was declined.

I was hoping he would plead not guilty so that I may have had an all-expenses paid trip to San Diego to give evidence – no such luck.

The silly man had burnt out his £4,500 car to no avail.

Such a simple crime to solve but then the importer must have been simple to think he could get away with it.

MORE ABOUT MERCEDES

After receiving another anonymous tip-off I had reason to be at Harwich Docks when three cars, two Mercedes and a BMW, all on Italian number plates came off the ferry. The three drivers were arrested and the cars impounded. The cars were later taken to our compound at Ascot whilst enquiries were made into their history.

It was quickly established that all three cars were on false Italian number plates but they were similar to those issued in Milan.

The men were bailed pending further enquiries.

Before charges could be preferred I had to establish that the cars were indeed stolen and obtain proof to support the criminal charges. I sent a telex via Interpol to the police at Milan informing them that the cars in my possession were on false Italian plates. I provided the cars chassis/VIN and engine numbers and asked that the theft be confirmed and statements be taken from the original owners.

As I had not received a reply, three weeks later another telex was sent to the Italian Police asking for an update on their enquiries.

Another three weeks went by and I at last received a reply, the Milan Police simply replied that the police in that country did not record the chassis/VIN and engine numbers of stolen vehicles so they could not help with the enquiry.

The three suspects bail was renewed again.

Contact was made with the Mercedes and BMW factories in Germany and they provided me with the names of the garages in Milan to whom the vehicles had been delivered.

Another telex via Interpol was sent to the Milan Police providing them with this additional information requesting visits be made to the two garages, details of the new owners ascertained and asking that statements be obtained from them.

Another month went by before I received a response the Milan Police tersely informed me that the information on the new cars held by the garages were subject to the Data Protection Act and therefore was not available.

The three suspects bail was yet again renewed.

By now I was getting frustrated by the poor response from the Milan Police then a bit of luck came my way. One of the Mercedes owners had made a warranty claim and the factory now had his personal details on file and the true Italian registration number.

Another telex message was sent to the Milan Police asking that the owner be interviewed confirming the ownership and theft and a statement obtained.

After a further two months had passed during which my follow up telex messages had not been replied to.

The three suspects bail was renewed, again.

A month later and some five and a half months from when my first request was sent to Milan I still had not received a reply.

I released the three suspects from their bail.

I was now in possession of three cars that were obviously stolen but I was not in a position to take the three suspects to court for stealing them.

I contacted the Custom and Excise at Harwich and they were delighted to relieve me of the cars. Under their terms of reference they could sell the cars as customs duty had not been paid on them and there was evidence the plates were false. This windfall would swell their coffers.

I had given up on this enquiry and then almost a year from my first telex to the Milan Police a totally inadequate statement from the Mercedes owner came through the post from the Milan Police. I binned it.

All of the communications between the Milan Police and myself had been made via Interpol.

Interpol in those days was like a police postal system and any enquiry received from overseas forces via Interpol that were of a motoring nature were directed to my office.

Instructions to my men were that all Interpol enquiries were dealt with promptly and efficiently as the reputation of the Thames Valley Police was reflected in the manner in which these enquiries were dealt with. Apparently, the Milan Police did not share the same view.

THE M4 CHEAT

There was a motor mechanic who worked at one of the motorway service stations on M4 motorway in Wiltshire.

He was such a nice man. He would go out of his way looking for oldish broken down vehicles on the M4 preferably with women or elderly drivers. He would be the epitome of the helpful mechanic, arrange for the car to be towed to the nearby service station and then organise onward transport for the stranded motorists, sometimes if they lived reasonably local in his own car.

A few days later he would then telephone the unfortunate owner and inform him or her that the car was suffering from a terminal illness and quoted a repair figure, allegedly provided by the garage at the service station, of an amount that was more than what the car was worth.

In reality the car had broken down due to some minor hiccup and the quote was not from the garage at all.

The car owner who probably lived some long distance away was confronted with a conundrum. What to do?

However help was at hand. The kindly mechanic knew of someone who would take the troublesome car off his or her hands for a small sum. That obliging person would also pay the towing in and storage fee. All lies of course.

As the go-between the mechanic would arrange for the payment of the money and receipt of the vehicle registration documents from the hapless motorist to the supposed new owner in reality the mechanic. What a nice man!

Once in the mechanic's possession a few pounds and a bit of his time spent on it and the car were ready for sale at a very reasonable profit.

His activities came to the notice of his manager who asked me to investigate. My experience was greater than his abilities to disguise his illegal acts. I traced at least eight cars he had so obtained.

He tried to bluff it out but my research had been too thorough and he eventually capitulated admitted to his sins and was immediately dismissed from his employ.

The mechanic was duly dealt with in the local Magistrates Court where he was sentenced to six months imprisonment.

CAR SECURITY

Ever since the motorcar was first invented the manufacturers have looked for ways to make their products secure against theft by villains who were inclined to make their living by stealing such cars.

We often liaised closely with the manufacturers. In fact we were occasionally asked to meet with the manufacturers to discuss matters concerning suggested vehicle security improvements.

Mercedes were one of the first European car manufacturers to introduce central locking. A system they thought would thwart the car thieves but within weeks of the first cars coming off the production line with the new technology they were being stolen. So how were the car thieves circumventing the new security system?

Easy.

The Mercedes central locking system worked on an air vacuum provided by the engine and the air vacuum tank situated inside the boot (trunk) just above the rear right wheel. The thieves with a long thin nail and hammer punched a hole right through the body panel over the rear wheel and into the vacuum tank puncturing it. All four door buttons then popped up giving the thief instant access.

The manufacturers had to rethink that problem.

When the remote locking system was introduced this was by far a better car security but again the thieves using a device called a 'grabber' soon overcame it.

The thief would sit in a car in a car park and when a nice and expensive car was parked nearby the grabber was switched on. It had a range of over fifty feet and as the owner of that lovely car operated the remote control to lock his car, the thief would operate his grabber and this device would record the remote controls electronic signal.

When the owner had left the scene, by operating a button on the grabber the doors of that nice car would be unlocked.

I firmly believe the car manufacturers will never be able to manufacture the ultimate thief proof car.

CARAVANS

During 1983 there was a large increase in the theft of caravans both in the Thames Valley area and nationally. This topic was bought up at the National Car Theft Conference at New Scotland Yard.

As a result of this, a Home Office Working Party was set up. This comprised of myself, a detective constable from Yorkshire Police and representatives of the National Caravan Council, the National Caravan Club, the DVLA, Swansea and a representative from the insurance industry. A senior civil servant from the Home Office was appointed to chair this working party.

The first meeting held at the Home Office was to discuss the general situation. As I looked around the room I noted that I was amongst some really high flyers at this meeting, a senior civil servant, the Chairman of the National Caravan Council, the President of the National Caravan Club, a senior official from the DVLA, and a high official from the Association of British Insurers, and myself a mere detective sergeant and a detective constable.

After a general discussion we were asked to go away and bring suggestions to the next meeting to improve caravan security and identification.

In those days Caravan identification was to it put it mildly pathetic. One manufacturer's identity was no more than a sticker outside and above the door that could easily be peeled off in seconds. The methods of identification were practically non-existent.

In preparation for the next meeting using a piece of green card I devised a CRD (Caravan Registration Document.) similar to the old vehicle registration book used for cars and other motor vehicles.

I folded the green card into three pages then using my own caravans identifying features as an example I typed on the first page the caravan's identification such as the country of manufacture, make, identifying numbers, colours, wheel plan, etc.

The second and third pages were to be used for the name of the supplying dealer, first, second and subsequent owners.

I then prepared a paper suggesting that the caravan manufacturers adopted a 17 digit CIN (Caravan Identification Number) similar to that used by the motor manufacturers VIN. Again using my own caravan as an example I devised a 17 digit CIN. The first digit denoting the name of country where the caravan was built, the second and third digit to denote the manufacturer, the fourth digit the model, the fifth digit the colour, sixth and seventh digit the year of manufacture, eighth digit where the caravan was built, the ninth digit would be a check number and the tenth to seventeenth digits would be a sequential number.

Secondly, I put forward a recommendation that the caravan manufacturers stamped a CIN (Caravan Identification Number) onto the caravan's 'A' frame and a supplementary number stamped onto a plate that was affixed elsewhere in the Caravan.

These proposals were not earth shattering or revolutionary and I was merely suggesting to the Working Party that caravan manufacturers adopted what the manufacturers of every other type of motor vehicle had been doing for many years.

At the next meeting I put forward my suggestions and was surprised to see that I was the only one who had given any thought to the problems we were collectively supposed to be resolving.

My suggestions were partly accepted but there was some opposition, particularly from the caravan manufacturer's representative who did not like the idea of the extra expense of stamping numbers and creating chassis plates.

The DVLA were reluctant to have records of caravans nationwide on their computer as in addition to motor vehicles they already had details on their Small Ships Register of boats not registered at Lloyds such as river boats, barges and launches.

I would have thought that if the DVLA had adopted my suggestion it would have generated more money for them so I could not understand their opposition. Once again politics and finance dictated and came before crime prevention and detection.

The suggestion of a Caravan Registration Document was watered down in that the caravan manufacturers included part of the CRD in the caravan handbook. At least it was something.

The caravan manufacturers did eventually adopt the stamping of the CIN on the 'A' frame and the fitting of an additional chassis plate. At last now there was a real chance that stolen caravans could be identified and restored to their rightful owners.

I was somewhat dismayed that none of the other committee members bothered to put any input into the discussions. Perhaps they were too highfaluting to be bothered with such mundane matters, leave it to the copper.

To sum up, where other members of the committee brought problems to the meeting I brought solutions.

OPERATION TABLET

As a sixteen year old I wanted to be like my two older brothers and become a hell raising motorcyclist so I sold my stamp collection for £7, saved £10 and with this vast amount of cash I bought an old, gutless and worn out BSA Bantam motorcycle. I was going to be a Hells Angel. Regrettably, I fell far short of that target.

When I had those youthful dreams way back in the late 1940s I was not to know that later in my life I would be heavily engaged with the Hells Angel movement, but not as a member.

My last major enquiry carried out whilst still in the police force was in connection with Operation Tablet. Initially, this operation was concerned solely with drugs hence the name but as information came in, it was obvious there was a far larger involvement with stolen motorcycles.

The operation commenced in December 1985 and by the time I retired in September 1986 my squads had recovered 104 stolen motorcycles of which fifty four were Harley Davidsons. Twenty five Hells Angels from the Reading area were arrested in connection with the thefts.

The method used to disguise the stolen motorcycles was simple and comparatively cheap to operate. One member of the Hells Angels made several visits to a Harley Davidson dealership in London and purchased minor parts for a Harley Davidson. He did not want the parts he wanted the sales receipts.

During this period of time photocopiers had been developed to such a standard that they could print off very good copies and the Hells Angels made full use of this advanced technology.

The Hells Angels would steal a Harley Davidson remove and dispose of the number plate alter one or two digits on the frame and engine numbers, then adjust the doctored receipts to show that all the parts required to make up a motorcycle had been purchased from the London dealer, engine, frame, tank, wheels, handlebars, seats, etc.

With these doctored sales receipts purporting that they had bought all of the parts necessary to make a whole motorcycle one of the Hells Angels would present the motorcycle to the Reading Taxation Office for registration.

As the machine was allegedly a built up machine it was allocated a 'Q' plate and a registration document. So registered, it was then advertised for sale thereby providing the Hells Angels with a huge profit.

To confuse matters further two or three motorcycles would be stolen and parts between the bikes interchanged some bikes were part resprayed and alterations made to the specification so that a motorcycle would appear as a different model altogether. It was a slick and well planned operation and had been going on for some years.

On the day that the operation was to take place over 250 police officers assembled at the Training Centre at Sulhamstead for a briefing at 3am in the morning. We had obtained search warrants for over 30 houses and premises in and around Reading.

At 5am that morning we descended on the premises. I recall one of their 'houses' in the Basingstoke Road where five or six Hells Angels lived, had a steel front door and just inside the door there was a six foot deep pit with metal spikes at the bottom.

They were ready for unwelcome visitors but were unprepared for our visit. Knowing about that premises security, two Ford Transit police vans were kitted out with ladders and platforms on the roof.

With policemen on the top of the van with battering rams they parked outside the premises tight against the wall. With a smash of glass teams of officers went through the first floor windows and inside the building within seconds.

All arrests were successfully carried out and then at our leisure my squads carried out searches and examination of their shops, garages, houses and other premises and we recovered a gold mine of evidence.

The whole operation was soured somewhat as the officer leading the enquiry wanted the men charged with conspiracy but the prosecuting solicitors deemed otherwise. Although good and solid evidence was obtained most of the Hells Angels escaped conviction at their trial.

Although I submitted several statements of evidence in relation to my examination and identification of the stolen motorcycles and a comprehensive report on my part in the raid, I was not called to give evidence in the trial that took place several months after I had retired from the police. I have no idea what happened to mess up what should have been a very successful operation.

THE CAR SQUAD, OLD AND NEW

When I retired from the police in September 1986 I left an efficient and very experienced Car Squad, so it was with some dismay that I heard a few months later the Car Squad had been disbanded

Who was there now in the force with the experience to unravel the complicated and very profitable (for the thieves) scams? Who had the knowledge about the complicated insurance frauds? Who could work out if a car had caught fire due to some electrical fault or if the fire had been deliberately set?

Surprisingly, now back in the 1980s I was asked to go on the selection board when vacancies came up on the car squad. I say surprisingly as in those days the selection board usually comprised of superintendents, so it was great that I, as a mere sergeant was asked to join them. On the other hand I was probably the only one with the technical knowledge to question the applicant as to his mechanical ability and knowledge of cars, motorcycles, lorries, plant, boats, caravans, etc.

The selection board had to turn down a young constable who was very knowledgeable on motor theft and who would have been suitable for the job, because he was not prepared to move house to join the Bracknell Squad.

At a social meeting in 2012 the same constable, now somewhat older, informed me that a few years after I had retired he put forward the suggestion that the car squad be reformed. His suggestion was accepted and a pilot scheme set up. However after a short period of time the powers that be decided that as this new squad, by turning up ringing gangs and those in other devious schemes relating to stolen vehicles were causing more problems than they were solving, the squad was again disbanded.

In some perverse way this new squads success was showing the force in a bad light and this is possibly why it was disbanded.

If what I was told was true, it reflects badly when the police were aware of major crime problems but would rather let sleeping dogs lie than deal with the problems head on.

VALUE FOR MONEY

When I left the Police Force I commenced employment as an Insurance Investigator for an international firm of loss adjusters. I was now dealing with a bewildering range of insurance frauds but still mainly dealing with vehicle claims.

About four years later I met up with an instructor from the Thames Valley Police Training Centre and he told me that since I retired lectures on auto crime were no longer part of the curriculum as there was no one qualified to give these lectures. I offered my services and obtained the permission of my employer to lecture free of charge. I then gave fortnightly lectures at the Force Training Centre at Sulhamstead, Berkshire for the next five years.

The lectures were well received thanks to good content and interesting visual aids. The lectures also received good ratings in the periodical critiques.

Occasionally, my lecture periods coincided with those of a coloured gentleman who originated in the West Indies and he talked on race relations. Sometimes we had lunch together in the training school restaurant so I knew that the police paid him a fat fee, travel expenses and he received a free lunch. I had to pay for mine.

In 1995 I retired from my employ and then informed the Training School that I was prepared to continue lecturing but please would they pay my travel expenses, about £25 per session. I was promptly dropped off the list of lecturers whereas I know the race relations' gentleman's services were retained.

I wonder how many crimes were solved, how many stolen vehicles were recovered and thieves arrested as a result of the information I had imparted over the five years, as compared to that from the man talking about race relations. I suppose it was a matter of priorities!

AND FINALLY

Well, that is it, I have run out of stories to tell but no doubt more stories will come to mind in due course, and you never know there may be a book three.

Policing is a very serious matter, dealing with natural and man-made disasters, death, serious crime, etc., so as an antidote police officers tend to develop a dark sense of humour.

I hope the stories I have related bring, if not a hearty laugh, then at least a smile to your face.

ABOUT THE AUTHOR

Now an octogenarian, Brian likes to keep up with the times, researching for books, already having produced four volumes of his family history.

His love of writing and stories in general has led him to publish his memoirs, in order that everyone may enjoy, or at least relive, some of the exploits of a young policeman in rural Buckinghamshire and surrounding areas.

Living in South Oxfordshire, Brian still enjoys a healthy and active lifestyle, playing badminton, cycling and trying to keep up with his four grandchildren.

Other books by Brian Wood

The Ramblings of a Rustic Copper

Published 2013

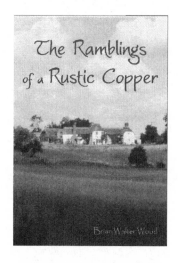

ISBN: 0957020236
ISBN-13: 978-0957020238

Made in the USA
Charleston, SC
26 December 2016